2209B: Expert Track: Updating Systems Administrator Skills from Microsoft® Windows® 2000 to Windows Server™ 2003

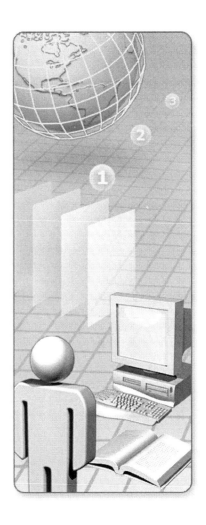

Information in this document, including URL and other Internet Web site references, is subject to change without notice. Unless otherwise noted, the example companies, organizations, products, domain names, e-mail addresses, logos, people, places, and events depicted herein are fictitious, and no association with any real company, organization, product, domain name, e-mail address, logo, person, place or event is intended or should be inferred. Complying with all applicable copyright laws is the responsibility of the user. Without limiting the rights under copyright, no part of this document may be reproduced, stored in or introduced into a retrieval system, or transmitted in any form or by any means (electronic, mechanical, photocopying, recording, or otherwise), or for any purpose, without the express written permission of Microsoft Corporation.

Microsoft may have patents, patent applications, trademarks, copyrights, or other intellectual property rights covering subject matter in this document. Except as expressly provided in any written license agreement from Microsoft, the furnishing of this document does not give you any license to these patents, trademarks, copyrights, or other intellectual property.

© 2003 Microsoft Corporation. All rights reserved.

Microsoft, MS-DOS, Windows, Windows NT, Windows Server 2003, Active Directory, MSDN, Windows Media, and Windows Server are either registered trademarks or trademarks of Microsoft Corporation in the U.S.A. and/or other countries.

The names of actual companies and products mentioned herein may be the trademarks of their respective owners.

Workshop: 2209B
Part Number: X10-00810
Released: 10/2003

END-USER LICENSE AGREEMENT FOR OFFICIAL MICROSOFT LEARNING PRODUCTS – STUDENT EDITION

PLEASE READ THIS END-USER LICENSE AGREEMENT ("EULA") CAREFULLY. BY USING THE MATERIALS AND/OR USING OR INSTALLING THE SOFTWARE THAT ACCOMPANIES THIS EULA (COLLECTIVELY, THE "LICENSED CONTENT"), YOU AGREE TO THE TERMS OF THIS EULA. IF YOU DO NOT AGREE, DO NOT USE THE LICENSED CONTENT.

1. **GENERAL.** This EULA is a legal agreement between you (either an individual or a single entity) and Microsoft Corporation ("Microsoft"). This EULA governs the Licensed Content, which includes computer software (including online and electronic documentation), training materials, and any other associated media and printed materials. This EULA applies to updates, supplements, add-on components, and Internet-based services components of the Licensed Content that Microsoft may provide or make available to you unless Microsoft provides other terms with the update, supplement, add-on component, or Internet-based services component. Microsoft reserves the right to discontinue any Internet-based services provided to you or made available to you through the use of the Licensed Content. This EULA also governs any product support services relating to the Licensed Content except as may be included in another agreement between you and Microsoft. An amendment or addendum to this EULA may accompany the Licensed Content.

2. **GENERAL GRANT OF LICENSE.** Microsoft grants you the following rights, conditioned on your compliance with all the terms and conditions of this EULA. Microsoft grants you a limited, non-exclusive, royalty-free license to install and use the Licensed Content solely in conjunction with your participation as a student in an Authorized Training Session (as defined below). You may install and use one copy of the software on a single computer, device, workstation, terminal, or other digital electronic or analog device ("Device"). You may make a second copy of the software and install it on a portable Device for the exclusive use of the person who is the primary user of the first copy of the software. A license for the software may not be shared for use by multiple end users. An "Authorized Training Session" means a training session conducted at a Microsoft Certified Technical Education Center, an IT Academy, via a Microsoft Certified Partner, or such other entity as Microsoft may designate from time to time in writing, by a Microsoft Certified Trainer (for more information on these entities, please visit www.microsoft.com). WITHOUT LIMITING THE FOREGOING, COPYING OR REPRODUCTION OF THE LICENSED CONTENT TO ANY SERVER OR LOCATION FOR FURTHER REPRODUCTION OR REDISTRIBUTION IS EXPRESSLY PROHIBITED.

3. **DESCRIPTION OF OTHER RIGHTS AND LICENSE LIMITATIONS**

    3.1 *Use of Documentation and Printed Training Materials.*

    3.1.1 The documents and related graphics included in the Licensed Content may include technical inaccuracies or typographical errors. Changes are periodically made to the content. Microsoft may make improvements and/or changes in any of the components of the Licensed Content at any time without notice. The names of companies, products, people, characters and/or data mentioned in the Licensed Content may be fictitious and are in no way intended to represent any real individual, company, product or event, unless otherwise noted.

    3.1.2 Microsoft grants you the right to reproduce portions of documents (such as student workbooks, white papers, press releases, datasheets and FAQs) (the "Documents") provided with the Licensed Content. You may not print any book (either electronic or print version) in its entirety. If you choose to reproduce Documents, you agree that: (a) use of such printed Documents will be solely in conjunction with your personal training use; (b) the Documents will not republished or posted on any network computer or broadcast in any media; (c) any reproduction will include either the Document's original copyright notice or a copyright notice to Microsoft's benefit substantially in the format provided below; and (d) to comply with all terms and conditions of this EULA. In addition, no modifications may made to any Document.

    Form of Notice:

    © 2003. Reprinted with permission by Microsoft Corporation. All rights reserved.

    Microsoft and Windows are either registered trademarks or trademarks of Microsoft Corporation in the US and/or other countries. Other product and company names mentioned herein may be the trademarks of their respective owners.

    3.2 *Use of Media Elements.* The Licensed Content may include certain photographs, clip art, animations, sounds, music, and video clips (together "Media Elements"). You may not modify these Media Elements.

    3.3 *Use of Sample Code.* In the event that the Licensed Content includes sample code in source or object format ("Sample Code"), Microsoft grants you a limited, non-exclusive, royalty-free license to use, copy and modify the Sample Code; if you elect to exercise the foregoing rights, you agree to comply with all other terms and conditions of this EULA, including without limitation Sections 3.4, 3.5, and 6.

    3.4 *Permitted Modifications.* In the event that you exercise any rights provided under this EULA to create modifications of the Licensed Content, you agree that any such modifications: (a) will not be used for providing training where a fee is charged in public or private classes; (b) indemnify, hold harmless, and defend Microsoft from and against any claims or lawsuits, including attorneys' fees, which arise from or result from your use of any modified version of the Licensed Content; and (c) not to transfer or assign any rights to any modified version of the Licensed Content to any third party without the express written permission of Microsoft.

3.5   *Reproduction/Redistribution Licensed Content.* Except as expressly provided in this EULA, you may not reproduce or distribute the Licensed Content or any portion thereof (including any permitted modifications) to any third parties without the express written permission of Microsoft.

4.   **RESERVATION OF RIGHTS AND OWNERSHIP.** Microsoft reserves all rights not expressly granted to you in this EULA. The Licensed Content is protected by copyright and other intellectual property laws and treaties. Microsoft or its suppliers own the title, copyright, and other intellectual property rights in the Licensed Content. You may not remove or obscure any copyright, trademark or patent notices that appear on the Licensed Content, or any components thereof, as delivered to you. **The Licensed Content is licensed, not sold.**

5.   **LIMITATIONS ON REVERSE ENGINEERING, DECOMPILATION, AND DISASSEMBLY.** You may not reverse engineer, decompile, or disassemble the Software or Media Elements, except and only to the extent that such activity is expressly permitted by applicable law notwithstanding this limitation.

6.   **LIMITATIONS ON SALE, RENTAL, ETC. AND CERTAIN ASSIGNMENTS.** You may not provide commercial hosting services with, sell, rent, lease, lend, sublicense, or assign copies of the Licensed Content, or any portion thereof (including any permitted modifications thereof) on a stand-alone basis or as part of any collection, product or service.

7.   **CONSENT TO USE OF DATA.** You agree that Microsoft and its affiliates may collect and use technical information gathered as part of the product support services provided to you, if any, related to the Licensed Content. Microsoft may use this information solely to improve our products or to provide customized services or technologies to you and will not disclose this information in a form that personally identifies you.

8.   **LINKS TO THIRD PARTY SITES.** You may link to third party sites through the use of the Licensed Content. The third party sites are not under the control of Microsoft, and Microsoft is not responsible for the contents of any third party sites, any links contained in third party sites, or any changes or updates to third party sites. Microsoft is not responsible for webcasting or any other form of transmission received from any third party sites. Microsoft is providing these links to third party sites to you only as a convenience, and the inclusion of any link does not imply an endorsement by Microsoft of the third party site.

9.   **ADDITIONAL LICENSED CONTENT/SERVICES.** This EULA applies to updates, supplements, add-on components, or Internet-based services components, of the Licensed Content that Microsoft may provide to you or make available to you after the date you obtain your initial copy of the Licensed Content, unless we provide other terms along with the update, supplement, add-on component, or Internet-based services component. Microsoft reserves the right to discontinue any Internet-based services provided to you or made available to you through the use of the Licensed Content.

10.   **U.S. GOVERNMENT LICENSE RIGHTS.** All software provided to the U.S. Government pursuant to solicitations issued on or after December 1, 1995 is provided with the commercial license rights and restrictions described elsewhere herein. All software provided to the U.S. Government pursuant to solicitations issued prior to December 1, 1995 is provided with "Restricted Rights" as provided for in FAR, 48 CFR 52.227-14 (JUNE 1987) or DFAR, 48 CFR 252.227-7013 (OCT 1988), as applicable.

11.   **EXPORT RESTRICTIONS**. You acknowledge that the Licensed Content is subject to U.S. export jurisdiction. You agree to comply with all applicable international and national laws that apply to the Licensed Content, including the U.S. Export Administration Regulations, as well as end-user, end-use, and destination restrictions issued by U.S. and other governments. For additional information see <http://www.microsoft.com/exporting/>.

12.   **TRANSFER.** The initial user of the Licensed Content may make a one-time permanent transfer of this EULA and Licensed Content to another end user, provided the initial user retains no copies of the Licensed Content. The transfer may not be an indirect transfer, such as a consignment. Prior to the transfer, the end user receiving the Licensed Content must agree to all the EULA terms.

13.   **"NOT FOR RESALE" LICENSED CONTENT.** Licensed Content identified as "Not For Resale" or "NFR," may not be sold or otherwise transferred for value, or used for any purpose other than demonstration, test or evaluation.

14.   **TERMINATION.** Without prejudice to any other rights, Microsoft may terminate this EULA if you fail to comply with the terms and conditions of this EULA. In such event, you must destroy all copies of the Licensed Content and all of its component parts.

15.   <u>**DISCLAIMER OF WARRANTIES.**</u> **TO THE MAXIMUM EXTENT PERMITTED BY APPLICABLE LAW, MICROSOFT AND ITS SUPPLIERS PROVIDE THE LICENSED CONTENT AND SUPPORT SERVICES (IF ANY)** *AS IS AND WITH ALL FAULTS,* **AND MICROSOFT AND ITS SUPPLIERS HEREBY DISCLAIM ALL OTHER WARRANTIES AND CONDITIONS, WHETHER EXPRESS, IMPLIED OR STATUTORY, INCLUDING, BUT NOT LIMITED TO, ANY (IF ANY) IMPLIED WARRANTIES, DUTIES OR CONDITIONS OF MERCHANTABILITY, OF FITNESS FOR A PARTICULAR PURPOSE, OF RELIABILITY OR AVAILABILITY, OF ACCURACY OR COMPLETENESS OF RESPONSES, OF RESULTS, OF WORKMANLIKE EFFORT, OF LACK OF VIRUSES, AND OF LACK OF NEGLIGENCE, ALL WITH REGARD TO THE LICENSED CONTENT, AND THE PROVISION OF OR FAILURE TO PROVIDE SUPPORT OR OTHER SERVICES, INFORMATION, SOFTWARE, AND RELATED CONTENT THROUGH THE LICENSED CONTENT, OR OTHERWISE ARISING OUT OF THE USE OF THE LICENSED CONTENT. ALSO, THERE IS NO WARRANTY OR CONDITION OF TITLE, QUIET ENJOYMENT, QUIET POSSESSION, CORRESPONDENCE TO DESCRIPTION OR NON-INFRINGEMENT WITH REGARD TO THE LICENSED CONTENT. THE ENTIRE RISK AS TO THE QUALITY, OR ARISING OUT OF THE USE OR PERFORMANCE OF THE LICENSED CONTENT, AND ANY SUPPORT SERVICES, REMAINS WITH YOU.**

16.   <u>**EXCLUSION OF INCIDENTAL, CONSEQUENTIAL AND CERTAIN OTHER DAMAGES**</u>**. TO THE MAXIMUM EXTENT PERMITTED BY APPLICABLE LAW, IN NO EVENT SHALL MICROSOFT OR ITS SUPPLIERS BE LIABLE FOR ANY SPECIAL, INCIDENTAL, PUNITIVE, INDIRECT, OR CONSEQUENTIAL DAMAGES WHATSOEVER (INCLUDING, BUT NOT**

LIMITED TO, DAMAGES FOR LOSS OF PROFITS OR CONFIDENTIAL OR OTHER INFORMATION, FOR BUSINESS INTERRUPTION, FOR PERSONAL INJURY, FOR LOSS OF PRIVACY, FOR FAILURE TO MEET ANY DUTY INCLUDING OF GOOD FAITH OR OF REASONABLE CARE, FOR NEGLIGENCE, AND FOR ANY OTHER PECUNIARY OR OTHER LOSS WHATSOEVER) ARISING OUT OF OR IN ANY WAY RELATED TO THE USE OF OR INABILITY TO USE THE LICENSED CONTENT, THE PROVISION OF OR FAILURE TO PROVIDE SUPPORT OR OTHER SERVICES, INFORMATION, SOFTWARE, AND RELATED CONTENT THROUGH THE LICENSED CONTENT, OR OTHERWISE ARISING OUT OF THE USE OF THE LICENSED CONTENT, OR OTHERWISE UNDER OR IN CONNECTION WITH ANY PROVISION OF THIS EULA, EVEN IN THE EVENT OF THE FAULT, TORT (INCLUDING NEGLIGENCE), MISREPRESENTATION, STRICT LIABILITY, BREACH OF CONTRACT OR BREACH OF WARRANTY OF MICROSOFT OR ANY SUPPLIER, AND EVEN IF MICROSOFT OR ANY SUPPLIER HAS BEEN ADVISED OF THE POSSIBILITY OF SUCH DAMAGES. BECAUSE SOME STATES/JURISDICTIONS DO NOT ALLOW THE EXCLUSION OR LIMITATION OF LIABILITY FOR CONSEQUENTIAL OR INCIDENTAL DAMAGES, THE ABOVE LIMITATION MAY NOT APPLY TO YOU.

17. **LIMITATION OF LIABILITY AND REMEDIES.** NOTWITHSTANDING ANY DAMAGES THAT YOU MIGHT INCUR FOR ANY REASON WHATSOEVER (INCLUDING, WITHOUT LIMITATION, ALL DAMAGES REFERENCED HEREIN AND ALL DIRECT OR GENERAL DAMAGES IN CONTRACT OR ANYTHING ELSE), THE ENTIRE LIABILITY OF MICROSOFT AND ANY OF ITS SUPPLIERS UNDER ANY PROVISION OF THIS EULA AND YOUR EXCLUSIVE REMEDY HEREUNDER SHALL BE LIMITED TO THE GREATER OF THE ACTUAL DAMAGES YOU INCUR IN REASONABLE RELIANCE ON THE LICENSED CONTENT UP TO THE AMOUNT ACTUALLY PAID BY YOU FOR THE LICENSED CONTENT OR US$5.00. THE FOREGOING LIMITATIONS, EXCLUSIONS AND DISCLAIMERS SHALL APPLY TO THE MAXIMUM EXTENT PERMITTED BY APPLICABLE LAW, EVEN IF ANY REMEDY FAILS ITS ESSENTIAL PURPOSE.

18. **APPLICABLE LAW.** If you acquired this Licensed Content in the United States, this EULA is governed by the laws of the State of Washington. If you acquired this Licensed Content in Canada, unless expressly prohibited by local law, this EULA is governed by the laws in force in the Province of Ontario, Canada; and, in respect of any dispute which may arise hereunder, you consent to the jurisdiction of the federal and provincial courts sitting in Toronto, Ontario. If you acquired this Licensed Content in the European Union, Iceland, Norway, or Switzerland, then local law applies. If you acquired this Licensed Content in any other country, then local law may apply.

19. **ENTIRE AGREEMENT; SEVERABILITY.** This EULA (including any addendum or amendment to this EULA which is included with the Licensed Content) are the entire agreement between you and Microsoft relating to the Licensed Content and the support services (if any) and they supersede all prior or contemporaneous oral or written communications, proposals and representations with respect to the Licensed Content or any other subject matter covered by this EULA. To the extent the terms of any Microsoft policies or programs for support services conflict with the terms of this EULA, the terms of this EULA shall control. If any provision of this EULA is held to be void, invalid, unenforceable or illegal, the other provisions shall continue in full force and effect.

Should you have any questions concerning this EULA, or if you desire to contact Microsoft for any reason, please use the address information enclosed in this Licensed Content to contact the Microsoft subsidiary serving your country or visit Microsoft on the World Wide Web at http://www.microsoft.com.

Si vous avez acquis votre Contenu Sous Licence Microsoft au CANADA :

DÉNI DE GARANTIES. Dans la mesure maximale permise par les lois applicables, le Contenu Sous Licence et les services de soutien technique (le cas échéant) sont fournis *TELS QUELS ET AVEC TOUS LES DÉFAUTS* par Microsoft et ses fournisseurs, lesquels par les présentes dénient toutes autres garanties et conditions expresses, implicites ou en vertu de la loi, notamment, mais sans limitation, (le cas échéant) les garanties, devoirs ou conditions implicites de qualité marchande, d'adaptation à une fin usage particulière, de fiabilité ou de disponibilité, d'exactitude ou d'exhaustivité des réponses, des résultats, des efforts déployés selon les règles de l'art, d'absence de virus et d'absence de négligence, le tout à l'égard du Contenu Sous Licence et de la prestation des services de soutien technique ou de l'omission de la 'une telle prestation des services de soutien technique ou à l'égard de la fourniture ou de l'omission de la fourniture de tous autres services, renseignements, Contenus Sous Licence, et contenu qui s'y rapporte grâce au Contenu Sous Licence ou provenant autrement de l'utilisation du Contenu Sous Licence. PAR AILLEURS, IL N'Y A AUCUNE GARANTIE OU CONDITION QUANT AU TITRE DE PROPRIÉTÉ, À LA JOUISSANCE OU LA POSSESSION PAISIBLE, À LA CONCORDANCE À UNE DESCRIPTION NI QUANT À UNE ABSENCE DE CONTREFAÇON CONCERNANT LE CONTENU SOUS LICENCE.

EXCLUSION DES DOMMAGES ACCESSOIRES, INDIRECTS ET DE CERTAINS AUTRES DOMMAGES. DANS LA MESURE MAXIMALE PERMISE PAR LES LOIS APPLICABLES, EN AUCUN CAS MICROSOFT OU SES FOURNISSEURS NE SERONT RESPONSABLES DES DOMMAGES SPÉCIAUX, CONSÉCUTIFS, ACCESSOIRES OU INDIRECTS DE QUELQUE NATURE QUE CE SOIT (NOTAMMENT, LES DOMMAGES À L'ÉGARD DU MANQUE À GAGNER OU DE LA DIVULGATION DE RENSEIGNEMENTS CONFIDENTIELS OU AUTRES, DE LA PERTE D'EXPLOITATION, DE BLESSURES CORPORELLES, DE LA VIOLATION DE LA VIE PRIVÉE, DE L'OMISSION DE REMPLIR TOUT DEVOIR, Y COMPRIS D'AGIR DE BONNE FOI OU D'EXERCER UN SOIN RAISONNABLE, DE LA NÉGLIGENCE ET DE TOUTE AUTRE PERTE PÉCUNIAIRE OU AUTRE PERTE

DE QUELQUE NATURE QUE CE SOIT) SE RAPPORTANT DE QUELQUE MANIÈRE QUE CE SOIT À L'UTILISATION DU CONTENU SOUS LICENCE OU À L'INCAPACITÉ DE S'EN SERVIR, À LA PRESTATION OU À L'OMISSION DE LA 'UNE TELLE PRESTATION DE SERVICES DE SOUTIEN TECHNIQUE OU À LA FOURNITURE OU À L'OMISSION DE LA FOURNITURE DE TOUS AUTRES SERVICES, RENSEIGNEMENTS, CONTENUS SOUS LICENCE, ET CONTENU QUI S'Y RAPPORTE GRÂCE AU CONTENU SOUS LICENCE OU PROVENANT AUTREMENT DE L'UTILISATION DU CONTENU SOUS LICENCE OU AUTREMENT AUX TERMES DE TOUTE DISPOSITION DE LA U PRÉSENTE CONVENTION EULA OU RELATIVEMENT À UNE TELLE DISPOSITION, MÊME EN CAS DE FAUTE, DE DÉLIT CIVIL (Y COMPRIS LA NÉGLIGENCE), DE RESPONSABILITÉ STRICTE, DE VIOLATION DE CONTRAT OU DE VIOLATION DE GARANTIE DE MICROSOFT OU DE TOUT FOURNISSEUR ET MÊME SI MICROSOFT OU TOUT FOURNISSEUR A ÉTÉ AVISÉ DE LA POSSIBILITÉ DE TELS DOMMAGES.

<u>LIMITATION DE RESPONSABILITÉ ET RECOURS.</u> MALGRÉ LES DOMMAGES QUE VOUS PUISSIEZ SUBIR POUR QUELQUE MOTIF QUE CE SOIT (NOTAMMENT, MAIS SANS LIMITATION, TOUS LES DOMMAGES SUSMENTIONNÉS ET TOUS LES DOMMAGES DIRECTS OU GÉNÉRAUX OU AUTRES), LA SEULE RESPONSABILITÉ 'OBLIGATION INTÉGRALE DE MICROSOFT ET DE L'UN OU L'AUTRE DE SES FOURNISSEURS AUX TERMES DE TOUTE DISPOSITION DEU LA PRÉSENTE CONVENTION EULA ET VOTRE RECOURS EXCLUSIF À L'ÉGARD DE TOUT CE QUI PRÉCÈDE SE LIMITE AU PLUS ÉLEVÉ ENTRE LES MONTANTS SUIVANTS : LE MONTANT QUE VOUS AVEZ RÉELLEMENT PAYÉ POUR LE CONTENU SOUS LICENCE OU 5,00 $US. LES LIMITES, EXCLUSIONS ET DÉNIS QUI PRÉCÈDENT (Y COMPRIS LES CLAUSES CI-DESSUS), S'APPLIQUENT DANS LA MESURE MAXIMALE PERMISE PAR LES LOIS APPLICABLES, MÊME SI TOUT RECOURS N'ATTEINT PAS SON BUT ESSENTIEL.

À moins que cela ne soit prohibé par le droit local applicable, la présente Convention est régie par les lois de la province d'Ontario, Canada. Vous consentez Chacune des parties à la présente reconnaît irrévocablement à la compétence des tribunaux fédéraux et provinciaux siégeant à Toronto, dans de la province d'Ontario et consent à instituer tout litige qui pourrait découler de la présente auprès des tribunaux situés dans le district judiciaire de York, province d'Ontario.

Au cas où vous auriez des questions concernant cette licence ou que vous désiriez vous mettre en rapport avec Microsoft pour quelque raison que ce soit, veuillez utiliser l'information contenue dans le Contenu Sous Licence pour contacter la filiale de succursale Microsoft desservant votre pays, dont l'adresse est fournie dans ce produit, ou visitez écrivez à : Microsoft sur le World Wide Web à http://www.microsoft.com

Contents

Introduction
- What Is a Workshop? 2
- Workshop Materials 3
- Prerequisites 4
- Workshop Outline 5
- Setup 7
- Microsoft Official Curriculum 8
- Microsoft Certified Professional Program 9
- Multimedia: Job Roles in Today's Information Systems Environment 12
- Facilities 13

Unit 1: Introduction to Systems Administration in Windows Server 2003
- Overview 1
- The Windows Server 2003 Family 2
- Administering Windows Server 2003 3
- Lab: Setting Up Your Administration Environment 4
- Lab Discussion 8

Unit 2: Managing Users, Computers, and Groups
- Overview 1
- Using Command-line Administration Tools 3
- Lab: Managing Users, Computers, and Groups 4
- Lab Discussion 11
- Best Practices for Managing Users 12
- Best Practices for Managing Computers and Groups 13

Unit 3: Using the GPMC to Manage Group Policy
- Overview 1
- What Is the Group Policy Management Console? 3
- Group Policy Modeling and Group Policy Results 4
- Lab: Using the GPMC to Manage Group Policy 5
- Lab Discussion 12
- Best Practices 14

Unit 4: Managing Resources and Security
- Overview 1
- Using Security Templates to Secure Your Network 2
- Lab: Managing Resources and Security 4
- Lab Discussion 9
- Best Practices 10

Unit 5: Managing DNS
- Overview 1
- What Are DNS Stub Zones? 3
- What Is Conditional Forwarding? 4
- Lab: Installing and Configuring DNS 6
- Lab Discussion 12
- Best Practices 13

Unit 6: Managing Servers
Overview 1
What is Remote Desktop for Administration? 2
Lab: Managing Servers 4
Lab Discussion 8
Best Practices 9

Unit 7: Managing Terminal Services
Overview 1
Terminal Server Licensing 2
Lab: Managing Terminal Services 4
Lab Discussion 8
Best Practices 9

Unit 8: Managing IIS 6.0 Web Services
Overview 1
What's New in IIS 6.0? 2
What are Application Pools? 4
Lab: Installing and Managing IIS 6.0 Web Services 6
Lab Discussion 11
Best Practices 12
Workshop Evaluation 14

Unit 9: Maintaining Software by Using Software Update Services
Overview 1
Multimedia: Software Update Services 2
Requirements for SUS 3
Lab: Maintaining Software by Using Software Update Services 5
Lab Discussion 9
Best Practices 10

Unit 10: Managing Disaster Recovery
Overview 1
Multimedia: Shadow Copies of Shared Folders 2
What Is Automated System Recovery? 3
Lab: Managing Disaster Recovery 4
Lab Discussion 8
Best Practices for Backing Up Data 9
Best Practices for Restoring Data 11
Workshop Evaluation 12

Appendix C: Network Files
Toolbox Resources

About This Workshop

This section provides you with a brief description of the workshop, audience, suggested prerequisites, and workshop objectives.

Description

This two-day instructor-led workshop provides students with the knowledge and skills to manage and maintain a Microsoft® Windows Server™ 2003 networked environment.

This discovery-based workshop consists primarily of labs that provide hands-on experience focused exclusively on the skills and objectives that align with Exam 70-292: *Managing and Maintaining a Microsoft Windows Server 2003 Environment for an MCSA Certified on Windows 2000*.

Audience

This workshop is intended for current Microsoft Windows® 2000 systems administrators and systems engineers who are currently at a skill level comparable to a 200-300 level learning experience. This audience must have experience managing and supporting a Windows 2000-based Active Directory® directory service-based network. The workshop is targeted specifically to students preparing for Exam 70-292: *Managing and Maintaining a Microsoft Windows Server 2003 Environment for an MCSA Certified on Windows 2000*.

Student Prerequisites

This workshop requires that students meet the following prerequisites:

- Hold either an MCSA on Windows 2000 or MCSE on Windows 2000 certification, or equivalent knowledge and skills.
- Have completed one of the following groups of courses to obtain equivalent knowledge and skills:
  - Course 2151, *Microsoft Windows 2000 Network and Operating System Essentials*
  - Course 2152, *Implementing Microsoft Windows 2000 Professional and Server*
  - Course 2126, *Managing a Microsoft Windows 2000 Network Environment*

    — or —

  - Course 2151, *Microsoft Windows 2000 Network and Operating System Essentials*
  - Course 2152, *Implementing Microsoft Windows 2000 Professional and Server*
  - Course 2153, *Implementing a Microsoft Windows 2000 Network Infrastructure*
  - Course 2154, *Implementing and Administering Microsoft Windows 2000 Directory Services*

Workshop Objectives

After completing this workshop, the student will be able to:

- Identify the systems administration tasks in Windows Server 2003 that are new or different from the tasks performed in Windows 2000.
- Manage user, computer, and group accounts in a Windows Server 2003 Active Directory-based environment.
- Use the Group Policy Management Console (GPMC) to manage Group Policy.
- Manage resources and security.
- Configure and manage DNS.
- Manage servers in remote locations.
- Manage Terminal Services.
- Manage IIS 6.0 Web services.
- Maintain computers that run Windows operating systems by implementing and managing Software Update Services.
- Prepare for and implement disaster recovery solutions.

Student Materials Compact Disc Contents

The Student Materials compact disc contains the following files and folders:

- *Autorun.exe*. When the compact disc is inserted into the CD-ROM drive, or when you double-click the **Autorun.exe** file, this file opens the compact disc and allows you to browse the Student Materials compact disc.

- *Autorun.inf*. When the compact disc is inserted into the compact disc drive, this file opens Autorun.exe.

- *Default.htm*. This file opens the Student Materials Web page. It provides you with resources pertaining to this workshop, including additional reading, review and lab answers, lab files, multimedia presentations, and workshop-related Web sites.

- *Readme.txt*. This file explains how to install the software for viewing the Student Materials compact disc and its contents and how to open the Student Materials Web page.

- *Addread*. This folder contains additional reading pertaining to this workshop.

- *Appendix*. This folder contains appendix files for this workshop.

- *Flash*. This folder contains the installer for the Macromedia Flash 6.0 browser plug-in.

- *Fonts*. This folder contains fonts that may be required to view the Microsoft Word documents that are included with this workshop.

- *Labfiles*. This folder contains files that are used in the hands-on labs. These files may be used to prepare the student computers for the hands-on labs.

- *Media*. This folder contains files that are used in multimedia presentations for this workshop.

- *Mplayer*. This folder contains the setup file to install Microsoft Windows Media™ Player.

- *Toolkit*. This folder contains the Resource Toolkit.

- *Webfiles*. This folder contains the files that are required to view the workshop Web page. To open the Web page, open Windows Explorer, and in the root directory of the compact disc, double-click **Default.htm** or **Autorun.exe**.

- *Wordview*. This folder contains the Word Viewer that is used to view any Word document (.doc) files that are included on the compact disc.

Document Conventions

The following conventions are used in workshop materials to distinguish elements of the text.

Convention	Use
📄	Represents Toolbox resources available by launching the Resource Toolkit shortcut on the desktop.
Bold	Represents commands, command options, and syntax that must be typed exactly as shown. It also indicates commands on menus and buttons, dialog box titles and options, and icon and menu names.
Italic	In syntax statements or descriptive text, indicates argument names or placeholders for variable information. Italic is also used for introducing new terms, for book titles, and for emphasis in the text.
Title Capitals	Indicate domain names, user names, computer names, directory names, and folder and file names, except when specifically referring to case-sensitive names. Unless otherwise indicated, you can use lowercase letters when you type a directory name or file name in a dialog box or at a command prompt.
ALL CAPITALS	Indicate the names of keys, key sequences, and key combinations—for example, ALT+SPACEBAR.
`monospace`	Represents code samples or examples of screen text.
[ ]	In syntax statements, enclose optional items. For example, [*filename*] in command syntax indicates that you can choose to type a file name with the command. Type only the information within the brackets, not the brackets themselves.
{ }	In syntax statements, enclose required items. Type only the information within the braces, not the braces themselves.
|	In syntax statements, separates an either/or choice.
▶	Indicates a procedure with sequential steps.
...	In syntax statements, specifies that the preceding item may be repeated.
. . .	Represents an omitted portion of a code sample.

Introduction

Contents

Introduction	1
What Is a Workshop?	2
Workshop Materials	3
Prerequisites	4
Workshop Outline	5
Setup	7
Microsoft Learning	8
Microsoft Certified Professional Program	9
Multimedia: Job Roles in Today's Information Systems Environment	12
Facilities	13

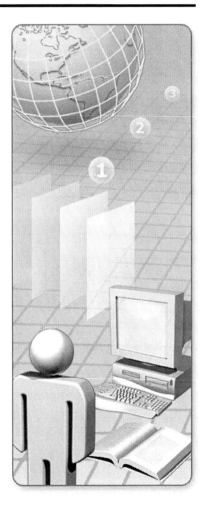

Information in this document, including URL and other Internet Web site references, is subject to change without notice. Unless otherwise noted, the example companies, organizations, products, domain names, e-mail addresses, logos, people, places, and events depicted herein are fictitious, and no association with any real company, organization, product, domain name, e-mail address, logo, person, place or event is intended or should be inferred. Complying with all applicable copyright laws is the responsibility of the user. Without limiting the rights under copyright, no part of this document may be reproduced, stored in or introduced into a retrieval system, or transmitted in any form or by any means (electronic, mechanical, photocopying, recording, or otherwise), or for any purpose, without the express written permission of Microsoft Corporation.

Microsoft may have patents, patent applications, trademarks, copyrights, or other intellectual property rights covering subject matter in this document. Except as expressly provided in any written license agreement from Microsoft, the furnishing of this document does not give you any license to these patents, trademarks, copyrights, or other intellectual property.

© 2003 Microsoft Corporation. All rights reserved.

Microsoft, MS-DOS, Windows, Windows NT, Windows Server 2003, Active Directory, MSDN, Windows Media, and Windows Server are either registered trademarks or trademarks of Microsoft Corporation in the United States and/or other countries.

The names of actual companies and products mentioned herein may be the trademarks of their respective owners.

Introduction

- Name
- Company affiliation
- Title/function
- Job responsibility
- Systems administration experience
- Windows operating systems experience
- Expectations for the workshop

What Is a Workshop?

- **A workshop provides:**
  - Fast-paced, hands-on learning
  - A learn-as-you-go environment
- **A workshop consists of:**
  - Lecture (minimal)
  - Scenario-based labs
  - Resource Toolkit

The workshop is a fast-paced learning format that favors labs over lecture. In a workshop, lecture time is kept to a minimum to give students the opportunity to focus on hands-on, scenario-based labs. The workshop format enables students to reinforce learning by doing and by problem solving.

Because lecture will focus only on the important or most difficult elements of a given topic, the labs include a Resource Toolkit that contains information like procedures, demonstrations, job aids, and other resources that are designed to give you the information you need to complete a lab. Your instructor is also a valuable resource for answering questions to help you complete the lab. The instructor will also lead discussions after the lab and review best practices.

Workshop Materials

- **Name card**
- **Student workbook**
- **Resource Toolkit**
- **Student Materials compact disc**
- **Workshop evaluation**
- **Evaluation software**

The following materials are included with your kit:

- *Name card.* Write your name on both sides of the name card.

- *Student workbook.* The student workbook contains the material covered in class, in addition to the hands-on lab exercises.

- *Resource Toolkit.* The Resource Toolkit is an online interface that contains resources that you will use in the scenario-based labs in this workshop. It includes video presentations, lab scenario information, and Toolbox resources—such as procedures and annotated screenshots—that will help you complete the labs. Most Toolbox resources are also printed in the *Resource Toolkit: Toolbox* book.

- *Student Materials compact disc.* The Student Materials compact disc contains the Web page that provides you with links to resources pertaining to this workshop, including additional readings, lab files, multimedia presentations, and workshop-related Web sites.

     Note To open the Web page, insert the Student Materials compact disc into the CD-ROM drive, and then in the root directory of the compact disc, double-click **Autorun.exe** or **Default.htm**.

- *Workshop evaluation.* To provide feedback on the workshop, training facility, and instructor, you will have the opportunity to complete an online evaluation near the end of the workshop.

    To provide additional comments or feedback on the workshop, send e-mail to support@mscourseware.com. To inquire about the Microsoft® Certified Professional program, send e-mail to mcphelp@microsoft.com.

- *Evaluation software.* An evaluation copy of the software is provided for your personal use only.

Prerequisites

- **MCSA on Windows 2000 or MCSE on Windows 2000 certification, or equivalent knowledge and skills**
- **Have completed one of the following groups of courses (or have equivalent knowledge and skills):**
  - Course 2151, *Windows 2000 Network and Operating System Essentials*
  - Course 2152, *Implementing Windows 2000 Professional and Server*
  - Course 2126, *Managing a Windows 2000 Network Environment*

  — or —

  - Course 2151, *Windows 2000 Network and Operating System Essentials*
  - Course 2152, *Implementing Windows 2000 Professional and Server*
  - Course 2153, *Implementing a Windows 2000 Network Infrastructure*
  - Course 2154, *Implementing and Administering Windows 2000 Directory Services*

This workshop requires that you meet the following prerequisites:

- Hold either an MCSA on Microsoft Windows® 2000 or MCSE on Windows 2000 certification, or equivalent knowledge and skills.

- Have completed one of the following groups of courses to obtain equivalent knowledge and skills:
  - Course 2151, *Microsoft Windows 2000 Network and Operating System Essentials*
  - Course 2152, *Implementing Microsoft Windows 2000 Professional and Server*
  - Course 2126, *Managing a Microsoft Windows 2000 Network Environment*

  — or —

  - Course 2151, *Microsoft Windows 2000 Network and Operating System Essentials*
  - Course 2152, *Implementing Microsoft Windows 2000 Professional and Server*
  - Course 2153, *Implementing a Microsoft Windows 2000 Network Infrastructure*
  - Course 2154, *Implementing and Administering Microsoft Windows 2000 Directory Services*

Workshop Outline

- Unit 1: Introduction to Systems Administration in Windows Server 2003
- Unit 2: Managing Users, Computers, and Groups
- Unit 3: Using the GPMC to Manage Group Policy
- Unit 4: Managing Resources and Security
- Unit 5: Managing DNS
- Unit 6: Managing Servers
- Unit 7: Managing Terminal Services
- Unit 8: Managing IIS 6.0 Web Services
- Unit 9: Maintaining Software by Using Software Update Services
- Unit 10: Managing Disaster Recovery

Unit 1, "Introduction to Systems Administration in Windows Server 2003," introduces the operating systems in the Microsoft Windows Server™ 2003 family and provides an overview of the systems administration tasks that you will perform in this workshop. After completing this unit, you will be able to identify the systems administration tasks in Windows Server 2003 that are new or different from the tasks performed in Windows 2000.

Unit 2, "Managing Users, Computers, and Groups," discusses the command-line administration tools that systems administrators can use to manage user, computer, and group accounts. After completing this unit, you will be able to manage user, computer, and group accounts in a Windows Server 2003 Active Directory® directory service-based environment.

Unit 3, "Using the GPMC to Manage Group Policy," introduces the new Group Policy Management Console (GPMC). After completing this unit, you will be able to use the GPMC to manage Group Policy in Windows Server 2003.

Unit 4, "Managing Resources and Security," reviews using security templates to secure computers in your network. In the lab, you will use the new effective permissions tool and change the owner of a folder; both which are new in Windows Server 2003. After completing this unit, you will be able to manage resources and security in Windows Server 2003.

Unit 5, "Managing DNS," introduces stub zones and conditional forwarding, which are new Domain Name System (DNS) features in Windows Server 2003. After completing this unit, you will be able to configure and manage DNS in Windows Server 2003.

Unit 6, "Managing Servers," introduces the tools in the new Remote Desktop for Administration feature in Windows Server 2003. After completing this unit, you will be able to manage servers in remote locations.

Unit 7, "Managing Terminal Services," discusses the new Terminal Server Licensing options available in Windows Server 2003. In the lab, you will install Terminal Services Licensing and use new Terminal Service settings in Group Policy. After completing this unit, you will be able to manage Terminal Services in Windows Server 2003.

Unit 8, "Managing IIS 6.0 Web Services," describes some of the new enhancements in Internet Information Service (IIS) 6.0, which is included in the operating systems in the Windows Server 2003 family. The unit also introduces application pooling, which helps ensure high availability for Web applications. After completing this unit, you will be able to install, configure, and manage IIS 6.0. Web services.

Unit 9, "Maintaining Software by Using Software Update Services," introduces Microsoft Software Update Services (SUS), a tool for managing and distributing software updates that resolve known security vulnerabilities and other stability issues in Windows 2000, Windows XP, and Windows Server 2003 operating systems. After completing this unit, you will be able to maintain computers that run Windows operating systems by implementing and managing SUS.

Unit 10, "Managing Disaster Recovery," introduces Volume Shadow Copy Service and Automated System Recovery, new features in Windows Server 2003 used for managing disaster recovery. After completing this unit, you will be able to prepare for and implement disaster recovery solutions in a Windows 2003-based network.

Setup

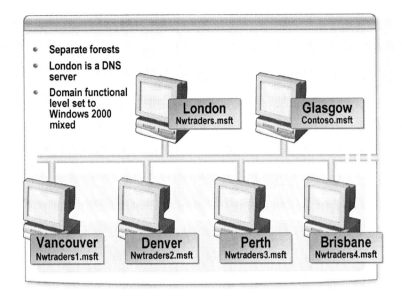

As you progress through this workshop, you will find it useful to understand how the classroom computers are configured.

Both instructor computers in the classroom are configured as domain controllers in their own forests:

- The primary instructor computer, called London, is in nwtraders.msft.
- The secondary instructor computer, called Glasgow, is in contoso.msft.

All student computers in the classroom:

- Are configured as domain controllers in their own forests called nwtraders$x$.msft, where x is the computer number assigned to each student.
- Use London as their DNS server.
- Have the domain functional level set to Windows 2000 mixed, which is the default for Windows Server 2003.

When administering servers, it is recommended that you log on to a trusted workstation and connect to the servers remotely. You should log on to the workstation as a non-administrator account and use Run As to run the administrator tools.

In this classroom setup, each student only has one computer so all administrative tasks can be performed only at the server console. To simulate a workstation environment and to allow you to practice using the **Run As** command as much as possible, your domain controller has been configured to allow all authenticated users to log on locally. This configuration also allows you to test your configurations with the only machine available to you. However, this is not a recommended security practice for a production environment.

Microsoft Learning

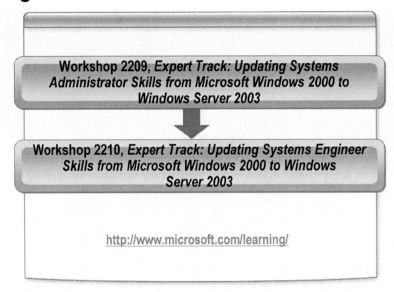

Microsoft Learning develops Official Microsoft Learning Products for computer professionals who design, develop, support, implement, or manage solutions by using Microsoft products and technologies. These learning products provide comprehensive skills-based training in instructor-led and online formats.

Additional Recommended Workshops

Each workshop relates in some way to another workshop. A related workshop may be a prerequisite, a follow-up workshop in a recommended series, or a workshop that offers additional training.

It is recommended that you take the following workshops in this order:

- Workshop 2209, *Expert Track: Updating Systems Administrator Skills from Microsoft Windows 2000 to Windows Server 2003*
- Workshop 2210, *Expert Track: Updating Systems Engineer Skills from Microsoft Windows 2000 to Windows Server 2003*

Other related courses and workshops may become available in the future, so for up-to-date information about recommended courses and workshops, visit the Microsoft Learning Web site.

Microsoft Learning Information

For more information, visit the Microsoft Learning Web site at http://www.microsoft.com/learning/.

Microsoft Certified Professional Program

Exam number and title	Core exam for the following track	Elective exam for the following track
70-292: *Managing and Maintaining a Windows Server 2003 Environment for an MCSA Certified on Windows 2000*	MCSA on Windows Server 2003	N/A

Microsoft CERTIFIED Professional

http://www.microsoft.com/learning/

Microsoft Learning offers a variety of certification credentials for developers and IT professionals. The Microsoft Certified Professional program is the leading certification program for validating your experience and skills, keeping you competitive in today's changing business environment.

Related Certification Exam

This workshop helps students to prepare for Exam 70-292: *Managing and Maintaining a Windows Server 2003 Environment* for an MCSA Certified on Windows 2000.

Exam 70-292 is the core exam for the MCSA on Windows Server 2003 certification. There are no additional core or elective exam requirements for an MCSA on Windows 2000 who passes exam 70-292.

MCP Certifications

The Microsoft Certified Professional program includes the following certifications.

- MCSA on Windows 2000 and MCSA on Windows Server 2003

    The Microsoft Certified Systems Administrator (MCSA) certification is designed for professionals who implement, manage, and troubleshoot existing network and system environments based on the Windows 2000 and Windows Server 2003 platforms. Implementation responsibilities include installing and configuring parts of the systems. Management responsibilities include administering and supporting the systems.

- MCSE on Windows 2000 and MCSE on Windows Server 2003

    The Microsoft Certified Systems Engineer (MCSE) credential is the premier certification for professionals who analyze the business requirements and design and implement the infrastructure for business solutions based on the Microsoft Windows 2000 and Windows Server 2003 platforms. Implementation responsibilities include installing, configuring, and troubleshooting network systems.

- MCAD

    The Microsoft Certified Application Developer (MCAD) for Microsoft .NET credential is appropriate for professionals who use Microsoft technologies to develop and maintain department-level applications, components, Web or desktop clients, or back-end data services or work in teams developing enterprise applications. The credential covers job tasks ranging from developing to deploying and maintaining these solutions.

- MCSD

    The Microsoft Certified Solution Developer (MCSD) credential is the premier certification for professionals who design and develop leading-edge business solutions with Microsoft development tools, technologies, platforms, and the Microsoft Windows DNA architecture. The types of applications MCSDs can develop include desktop applications and multi-user, Web-based, N-tier, and transaction-based applications. The credential covers job tasks ranging from analyzing business requirements to maintaining solutions.

- MCDBA on Microsoft SQL Server™ 2000

    The Microsoft Certified Database Administrator (MCDBA) credential is the premier certification for professionals who implement and administer Microsoft SQL Server databases. The certification is appropriate for individuals who derive physical database designs, develop logical data models, create physical databases, create data services by using Transact-SQL, manage and maintain databases, configure and manage security, monitor and optimize databases, and install and configure SQL Server.

- MCP

    The Microsoft Certified Professional (MCP) credential is for individuals who have the skills to successfully implement a Microsoft product or technology as part of a business solution in an organization. Hands-on experience with the product is necessary to successfully achieve certification.

- MCT

    Microsoft Certified Trainers (MCTs) demonstrate the instructional and technical skills that qualify them to deliver Microsoft Learning through Microsoft Certified Technical Education Centers (Microsoft CTECs).

Certification Requirements

The certification requirements differ for each certification category and are specific to the products and job functions addressed by the certification. To become a Microsoft Certified Professional, you must pass rigorous certification exams that provide a valid and reliable measure of technical proficiency and expertise.

 Additional Information See the Microsoft Learning Web site at http://www.microsoft.com/learning/.

You can also send e-mail to mcphelp@microsoft.com if you have specific certification questions.

Acquiring the Skills Tested by an MCP Exam

Official Microsoft Learning Products can help you develop the skills that you need to do your job. They also complement the experience that you gain while working with Microsoft products and technologies. However, no one-to-one correlation exists between Microsoft Learning course or workshops and MCP exams. Microsoft does not expect or intend for a course or workshop to be the sole preparation method for passing MCP exams. Practical product knowledge and experience is also necessary to pass the MCP exams.

To help prepare for the MCP exams, use the preparation guides that are available for each exam. Each Exam Preparation Guide contains exam-specific information, such as a list of the topics on which you will be tested. These guides are available on the Microsoft Learning Web site at http://www.microsoft.com/learning/.

Multimedia: Job Roles in Today's Information Systems Environment

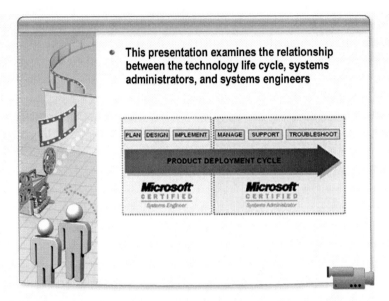

To view the *Job Roles in Today's Information Systems Environment* presentation, open the Web page on the Student Materials compact disc, click **Multimedia**, and then click the title of the presentation. After you open the multimedia presentation, press F11 to view it in full-screen mode. Do not open this presentation unless your instructor tells you to.

Facilities

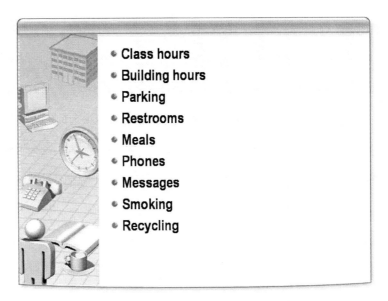

- Class hours
- Building hours
- Parking
- Restrooms
- Meals
- Phones
- Messages
- Smoking
- Recycling

Unit 1: Introduction to Systems Administration in Windows Server 2003

Contents

Overview	1
The Windows Server 2003 Family	2
Administering Windows Server 2003	3
Lab: Setting Up Your Administration Environment	4
Lab Discussion	8

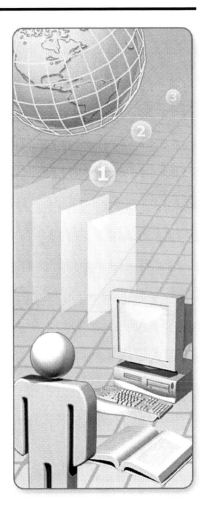

Information in this document, including URL and other Internet Web site references, is subject to change without notice. Unless otherwise noted, the example companies, organizations, products, domain names, e-mail addresses, logos, people, places, and events depicted herein are fictitious, and no association with any real company, organization, product, domain name, e-mail address, logo, person, place or event is intended or should be inferred. Complying with all applicable copyright laws is the responsibility of the user. Without limiting the rights under copyright, no part of this document may be reproduced, stored in or introduced into a retrieval system, or transmitted in any form or by any means (electronic, mechanical, photocopying, recording, or otherwise), or for any purpose, without the express written permission of Microsoft Corporation.

Microsoft may have patents, patent applications, trademarks, copyrights, or other intellectual property rights covering subject matter in this document. Except as expressly provided in any written license agreement from Microsoft, the furnishing of this document does not give you any license to these patents, trademarks, copyrights, or other intellectual property.

© 2003 Microsoft Corporation. All rights reserved.

Microsoft, MS-DOS, Windows, Windows NT, Windows Server 2003, Active Directory, MSDN, Windows Media, and Windows Server are either registered trademarks or trademarks of Microsoft Corporation in the United States and/or other countries.

The names of actual companies and products mentioned herein may be the trademarks of their respective owners.

Overview

- **The Windows Server 2003 Family**
- **Administering Windows Server 2003**
- **Lab: Setting Up Your Administration Environment**

Within the spectrum of administration tasks performed by systems administrators, Microsoft® Windows Server™ 2003 provides new capabilities and tools for centrally managing an organization's users, computers, and network resources. Although the systems administrator's job role covers a broad spectrum of these tasks, this workshop will focus on the administration tasks that are affected by new features in the operating systems in the Windows Server 2003 family.

Objectives

After completing this unit, you will be able to:

- Identify the products in the Windows Server 2003 family.
- Identify the systems administration tasks in Windows Server 2003 that are addressed in this workshop.
- Identify the tools and resources available to perform the tasks in this workshop.

The Windows Server 2003 Family

	Web Edition	Standard Edition	Enterprise Edition	Datacenter Edition
Processors	2	4	8	32/64*
Memory	2 GB	4 GB	32 GB / 64 GB*	64 GB / 512 GB*
Domain controller?	No	Yes	Yes	Yes
Clustering support	No	No	8-node	8-node
64-bit support	No	No	Yes	Yes

* 64-bit version

Windows Server 2003 is available in four different editions. Each edition is designed to be used in a specific server role. This enables you to select the operating system edition that provides the functions and capabilities that meets the needs of your organization.

- *Windows Server 2003, Web Edition.* Designed to be used as a Web server. It is available only through selected partner channels and is not available for retail sale. Although computers running this version can be members of an Active Directory® directory service domain, you cannot configure a computer running Windows Server 2003, Web Edition as a domain controller.

- *Windows Server 2003, Standard Edition.* Designed for small organizations and departmental use. Use Windows Server 2003, Standard Edition for domain controllers and member servers and when your server does not require the increased hardware support and clustering features of Windows Server 2003, Enterprise Edition.

- *Windows Server 2003, Enterprise Edition.* Designed for use in medium and large organizations as application servers, domain controllers, and for clustering. Includes all the features in Windows Server 2003, Standard Edition; the primary difference between Windows Server 2003, Enterprise Edition, and Windows Server 2003, Standard Edition, is that Enterprise Edition supports high-performance servers, and is recommended for servers running applications for networking, messaging, inventory and customer service systems, databases, and e-commerce Web sites.

- *Windows Server 2003, Datacenter Edition.* Designed to provide the highest levels of scalability and availability. Use for mission-critical solutions for databases, enterprise resource planning software, high-volume real-time transaction processing, and server consolidation. The primary difference between Windows Server 2003, Datacenter Edition, and Windows Server 2003, Enterprise Edition, is that Datacenter Edition supports more powerful multiprocessing and greater memory capacity. In addition, Windows Server 2003, Datacenter Edition, is available only through the Windows Datacenter Program offered to Original Equipment Manufacturers (OEMs).

 Additional Information For detailed information about each edition's capabilities, see the product overviews on the Windows Server 2003 page at http://www.microsoft.com/windowsserver2003/.

Administering Windows Server 2003

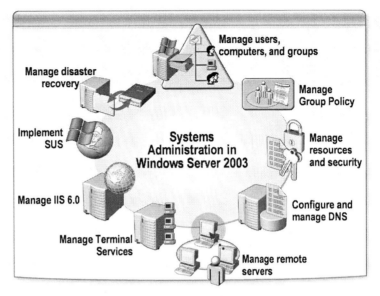

Systems administrators with experience managing and supporting a Microsoft Windows® 2000-based network can apply those skills in a network environment based on Windows Server 2003 by using new tools to perform common administration tasks. Additionally, experienced systems administrators will be able to quickly learn administration tasks that are new in Windows Server 2003.

The following administration tasks are affected by new tools and capabilities in Windows Server 2003:

- Manage user, computer, and group accounts in an Active Directory-based environment.
- Use the Group Policy Management Console (GPMC) to manage Group Policy.
- Manage resources and security.
- Configure and manage DNS.
- Manage servers in remote locations.
- Manage Terminal Services.
- Manage IIS 6.0 Web servers.
- Maintain computers that run Windows operating systems by implementing and managing Software Update Services.
- Prepare for and implement disaster recovery solutions.

 Additional Information For information about the systems administration tasks performed in Windows Server 2003, see Appendix A, "Differences Between Microsoft Windows Server 2003 and Microsoft Windows 2000" in Workshop 2209, *Expert Track: Updating Systems Administrator Skills from Microsoft Windows 2000 to Windows Server 2003*.

Lab: Setting Up Your Administration Environment

In this lab, you will:
- Use the Resource Toolkit
- Create a regular user account
- Use Run As to run administrative tools

After completing this lab, you will be able to:

- Use the Resource Toolkit.
- Create a regular user account.
- Use Run As to run administrative tools with elevated privileges.

Toolbox Resources

If necessary, use one or more of the following Toolbox resources to help you complete this lab:

- Using the Workshop Resources
- Using the Run As Command
- Guidelines for Creating Strong Passwords
- Accessing the Administrative Tools from a Non-Administrator Account

Estimated time to complete this lab: **15 minutes**

Exercise 1
Setting Up Your Environment and Exploring the Resource Toolkit

In this exercise, you will set up your administration environment for this workshop. You will also learn how to use the different components in the Resource Toolkit.

Tasks	Supporting information
1. Log on as Administrator and read the e-mail from Maria.	■ The current server password is P@ssw0rd. ■ You can access the Resource Toolkit by using the icon on your desktop. ■ As you work through each step, in addition to offering tips, the Supporting information column will recommend resources to help you. For example, if you aren't sure what a strong password is, you can use a resource listed on the **Toolbox** tab in the Resource Toolkit. If you already know what to do, you don't need to use the Toolbox resource. See the Toolbox resource, Using the Workshop Resources.
2. Locate the company security policies and read *Acceptable Use of Administrator and Non-Administrator Accounts* and *Account Creation Policy*.	■ Sometimes the same resource will be recommended for a similar task. See the Toolbox resource, Using the Workshop Resources.
3. Set a strong password on the Administrator account. **Note:** To facilitate classroom management, please write down your new Administrator password and give it to the instructor. You do not need to share this password with the other students.	■ See the company security policy, Acceptable Use of Administrator and non-Administrator Accounts in the Network Files folder. See the Toolbox resource, Guidelines for Creating Strong Passwords.
4. Create a regular user account for yourself. You will use this account during this workshop.	■ Use a name that follows company naming conventions. See the company policy, Account Creation Policy in the Network Files folder. ■ Tasks that have not changed significantly since Windows 2000 Server will not have Toolbox resources but may have tips or additional information to help you complete the task.
5. Log on by using your non-administrator account and access an administrative tool by using Run As from the shortcut menu.	See the following Toolbox resources: ■ Accessing the Administrative Tools from a Non-Administrator Account ■ Using the Run As command

(*continued*)

Tasks	Supporting information

6. Be prepared to complete the rest of the administrative tasks that Maria assigns to you.	■ To complete these tasks you could:
	   • Log on as an administrator.
	   • Remain logged on with a non-administrator account and use Run As.
	■ Decide which approach is the best solution, and then implement it. You can use the space below to record your decision. Be prepared to explain your decision.
	
	_____
	_____
	_____
	_____

Lab E-mail

From: Maria Hammond

To: Systems Administrators

Sent: Thu Aug 21 19:38:19 2003

Subject: NorthWind Traders security policies

I wanted to make sure you understand a few things. Security is very important to us. I would like you to take a few minutes and locate our company security policies. You'll find them in the Network Files folder. You will be held accountable for upholding these security policies. Start by reading Acceptable use of administrator and non-administrator accounts and Account creation policy.

For now, you'll be in charge of your own domain and domain controller. My assistant will tell you the current password. Please set a new strong password for the Administrator account and let my assistant know what it is, as specified in the company security policies. Please create a regular user account for yourself and use that account unless you must be logged on as the administrator. Use the Run As command to access the Administrator account in all other cases. Failing to comply with this policy can have a serious negative impact on your performance review.

Thanks for your cooperation.

Maria Hammond, MCSE

Network Manager

NorthWind Traders, Inc.

Lab Discussion

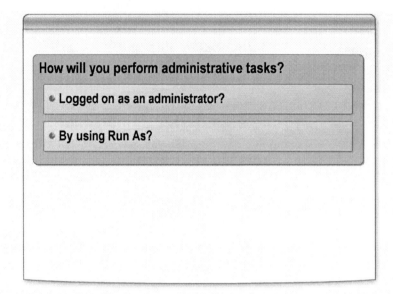

Discuss with the class how you implemented the solutions in the preceding lab. During this discussion, explain why you chose a particular solution.

- How will you perform the administrative tasks for the remainder of the workshop? Will you:
  - Log on as an administrator?
  - Log on with a non-administrator account and use Run As?

Unit 2: Managing Users, Computers, and Groups

Contents

Overview	1
Using Command-line Administration Tools	3
Lab: Managing Users, Computers, and Groups	4
Lab Discussion	11
Best Practices for Managing Users	12
Best Practices for Managing Computers and Groups	13

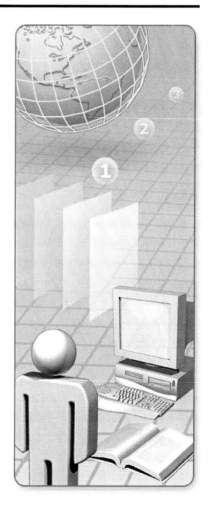

Information in this document, including URL and other Internet Web site references, is subject to change without notice. Unless otherwise noted, the example companies, organizations, products, domain names, e-mail addresses, logos, people, places, and events depicted herein are fictitious, and no association with any real company, organization, product, domain name, e-mail address, logo, person, place or event is intended or should be inferred. Complying with all applicable copyright laws is the responsibility of the user. Without limiting the rights under copyright, no part of this document may be reproduced, stored in or introduced into a retrieval system, or transmitted in any form or by any means (electronic, mechanical, photocopying, recording, or otherwise), or for any purpose, without the express written permission of Microsoft Corporation.

Microsoft may have patents, patent applications, trademarks, copyrights, or other intellectual property rights covering subject matter in this document. Except as expressly provided in any written license agreement from Microsoft, the furnishing of this document does not give you any license to these patents, trademarks, copyrights, or other intellectual property.

© 2003 Microsoft Corporation. All rights reserved.

Microsoft, MS-DOS, Windows, Windows NT, Windows Server 2003, Active Directory, MSDN, Windows Media, and Windows Server are either registered trademarks or trademarks of Microsoft Corporation in the United States and/or other countries.

The names of actual companies and products mentioned herein may be the trademarks of their respective owners.

Overview

- Using Command-line Administration Tools
- Lab: Managing Users, Computers, and Groups
- Lab Discussion
- Best Practices for Managing Users
- Best Practices for Managing Computers and Groups

Active Directory Users and Computers is the primary tool used to manage users, computers, and groups in Microsoft® Windows Server™ 2003. New features in Active Directory Users and Computers include the capability to:

- Move objects by using a drag-and-drop operation.
- Modify properties for multiple accounts.
- Create and save queries to find Active Directory® directory service objects.

Additionally, Windows Server 2003 also provides new command line tools to perform common administrative tasks.

Objectives

After completing this unit, you will be able to:

- Create user accounts by using the **dsadd** command.
- Create computer accounts by using the **dsadd** command.
- Create groups by using the **dsadd** command.
- Add members to a group by using the **dsmod** command.
- Copy the properties from an existing account when creating a new account.
- Modify the properties of multiple accounts by using:
  - The multi-select feature in Active Directory Users and Computers.
  - The **dsmod** command.
- Find Active Directory objects by using:
  - Common queries.
  - Saved queries.
  - The **dsquery** command.
- Move an Active Directory object by using a drag-and-drop operation in Active Directory Users and Computers.
- Reset computer accounts.
- Determine the effective permissions on an Active Directory object.

Using Command-line Administration Tools

- **New administrative commands in Windows Server 2003**
  - **dsadd**—Create users, computers, and groups
  - **dsmod**—Modify account properties and add members to groups
  - **dsquery**—Find Active Directory objects
- **Configure commands in batch files to perform tasks for multiple accounts**
- **Benefits of using command-line tools**
  - Automate common administrative tasks
  - Easier to manage large numbers of accounts
  - Reduce human error
  - Convenient for administrators who prefer to use the command line

---

- The new administrative commands in Window Server 2003 include the following commands:
  - **dsadd**—Use to create users, computers, groups and other Active Directory objects.
  - **dsmod**—Use to modify account properties, add members to groups, and make changes to other Active Directory objects.
  - **dsquery**—Use to find Active Directory objects.
- You can collect multiple instances of commands in a batch file to automate administrative tasks. To create a batch file, copy or type each command into a text file, and then save the file with a .cmd file extension.
- The benefits of using command-line tools to perform administrative tasks include:
  - Automating common administrative tasks.
  - Making it easier to manage large numbers of accounts.
  - Reducing time and human error when managing large numbers of accounts.
  - Convenience for administrators who prefer to use the command line.

 Tip For more information about **dsadd**, **dsmod**, or **dsquery**, at a command prompt, type one of the following commands:

dsadd /?

dsmod /?

dsquery /?

Lab: Managing Users, Computers, and Groups

In this lab, you will:
- Create and manage user, computer, and group accounts
- Troubleshoot user logon problems

After completing this lab, you will be able to:

- Create and manage user, computer, and group accounts.
- Troubleshoot user logon problems.

Toolbox Resources

If necessary, use one or more of the following Toolbox resources to help you complete this lab:

- Using **dsadd** to Create User Accounts
- Using CSVDE to Create User Accounts
- Using **dsmod** to Modify User Accounts
- Group Strategy Review
- Using **dsadd** to Create Groups
- Using **dsmod** to Add Members to a Group
- User Account Properties Copied from an Existing to a New Account
- Using **dsadd** to Create Computer Accounts
- Modifying Properties for Multiple User Accounts
- Using Common Queries to Find Active Directory Objects
- Creating a Saved Query to Find Locked-out Accounts
- Issues with Resetting Passwords
- How to Verify the Effective Permissions for Managing an Active Directory Object

Estimated time to complete this lab: **75 minutes**

Exercise 1
Managing User, Computer, and Group Accounts

In this exercise, you will create and manage user accounts by using both graphical and command-line tools.

Tasks	Supporting information
1. Create accounts for the new users specified in Maria's e-mail message.	**Tip:** You can copy and paste names from Maria's e-mail messages. ■ Ensure that accounts are named according to company policy. ■ There are several ways that you can create these user accounts: • Manually, by using Active Directory Users and Computers • By using a batch file with the **dsadd user** command • By creating a CSV file, and then importing it by using the **csvde** command ■ Decide which approach is the best solution, and then implement it. You can use the space below to record your decision. Be prepared to explain your solution. See the following Toolbox resources: ■ Using Dsadd to Create User Accounts ■ Using Csvde to Create User Accounts
2. Create groups, as described in Maria's email. Add users and groups to the groups in which they belong.	■ Ensure that groups are named according to company policy. ■ There are several ways that you can create these groups and populate them: • Manually, by using Active Directory Users and Computers • By using a batch file with the **dsadd group** command • By using the dsmod group command ■ Decide which approach is the best solution, and then implement it. You can use the space below to record your decision. Be prepared to explain your solution. See the following Toolbox resources: ■ Using Dsadd to Create Groups ■ Group Strategy Review ■ Using Dsmod to Add Members to a Group

(continued)

Tasks	Supporting information
3. Make three new phone rep manager accounts like the Holly Holt user account, but with different phone extensions. Plan for the creation of future phone rep managers. • Ken Kwok (x2274) • Danielle Tiedt (x2810) • Florian Voss (x2210)	▪ What is the most efficient way to do this? See the Toolbox resource, User Account Properties Copied from an Existing to a New Account.
4. Grant all CSO users Modify access to the C:\CSO folder.	▪ There are several ways that you can assign these permissions: • By assigning rights directly to the individual users • By assigning rights to the existing group accounts • By assigning rights to a new group that you create to contain all CSO users
5. Create a computer named *user*1 for each user listed in Maria's e-mail. Create them in the same organizational unit as the user.	▪ Follow the naming convention *user*1, as described in Maria's e-mail. See the Toolbox resource, Using Dsadd to Create Computer Accounts.
6. Change the fax number for all of the existing users in the CSO organizational unit to 555-555-1212.	▪ There are two ways you can modify user accounts: • By using Active Directory Users and Computers • By using the **dsmod user** command ▪ Decide which approach is the best solution, and then implement it. You can use the space below to record your decision. Be prepared to explain your solution. _____ _____ _____ See the following Toolbox resources: ▪ Modifying Properties for Multiple User Accounts ▪ Using Dsmod to Modify User Accounts
7. Find accounts that do not have the password set to expire, and then clear that setting. Then, find and unlock Bjorn Rettig's account by searching for locked accounts. Move Bjorn's account to the CSO organizational unit.	▪ There are several ways you can find the users: • By using a common query • By using a pre-existing saved query See the following Toolbox resources: ▪ Using Common Queries to Find Active Directory Objects ▪ Creating a Saved Query to Find Locked-out Accounts

Exercise 2
Troubleshooting User Account Problems

In this exercise, you will troubleshoot the problems described in the following table.

Issues	Supporting information
1. John Rodman, is unable to log on because he has forgotten his password. Resolve the problem.	■ For a hint, see the Toolbox resource, Troubleshooting User Account Problems. See the Toolbox resource, Issues with Resetting Passwords.
2. Mary Baker cannot log on to the computer bakerm1. Diagnose and fix the problem.	■ For a hint, see the Toolbox resource, Troubleshooting User Account Problems.
3. Bjorn Rettig is attempting to move Peter Houston's account from the HR organizational unit to the CSO organizational unit. Bjorn is receiving the error "Windows cannot move object Peter Houston because: access to the object is denied." Diagnose the problem, but do not fix it.	■ For a hint, see the Toolbox resource, Troubleshooting User Account Problems. See the Toolbox resource, How to Verify the Effective Permissions for Managing an Active Directory Object.

Lab E-mail 1

From: Maria Hammond

To: Systems Administrators

Sent: Thu Aug 21 20:49:33 2003

Subject: CSO reorganization

Hi,

As I told you, there are several users who used to work for our subsidiary who will be working directly for us effective one week from today. We'll need to create user accounts for them in the CSO organizational unit. I'll send you those accounts in a separate e-mail. It will also include the groups they should belong to. Please refer to the company policies for user name creation and passwords.

- Each user will have a computer named username1. They should be created in the same organizational unit as the user.
- There are several existing users in the CSO organizational unit. All of the existing users in the CSO organizational unit need to have their fax number changed to 555-555-1212.
- We had some problems in the past with users in CSO having passwords that don't expire. If you find any, please change those accounts.

One last thing - Bjorn Rettig's account is locked out. Can you please unlock his account and move it to the CSO organizational unit? I don't remember what organizational unit he's currently in.

These employees won't be starting until next week, so if you don't get around to creating them all today, that's fine. Just get started and let me know if you're having any problems.

Maria Hammond, MCSE

Network Manager

NorthWind Traders, Inc.

Lab E-mail 2

From: Maria Hammond

To: Systems Administrators

Sent: Thu Aug 21 20:54:09 2003

Subject: Users for CSO reorganization

Here's the list of users you need to create. They'll be starting one week from today.

All of the new users should be in security groups according to their job functions. These users will need to have Modify permissions to the CSO files on all of the CSO servers. Please create groups accordingly. Refer to the company policy on group naming conventions.

Phone reps

- Blue, Kelly bluek
- Ben-Sachar, Ido bensachari
- Fluegel, Jay fluegelj
- Grande, Jon grandej
- Hankin, Alex hankina
- Jiang, George jiangg
- Kelly, Robert kellyr
- Kelly, Bob kellyb
- Li, Yuhong liy
- Moreland, Barbara morelandb
- Naik, Mandar naikm
- O'Donnell, Claire odonnellc
- Smith, John smithj

CSO Managers

- Ciccu, Alice ciccua
- Su, Min sum

Admin assistants

- Lugo, Jose lugoj
- Ito, Shu itos

We're also going to have 3 new phone rep managers starting soon:

- Kwok, Ken kwokk (extension 2274)
- Tiedt, Danielle tiedtd (extension 2810)
- Voss, Florian vossf (extension 2210)

Take a look at the Holly Holt account and make those accounts just like it except for their phone extensions as shown above. We'll be hiring several more phone rep managers in the next few months.

Maria Hammond, MCSE

Network Manager

NorthWind Traders, Inc.

Lab Discussion

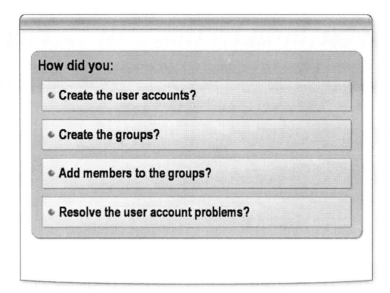

Discuss with the class how you implemented the solutions in the preceding lab. During this discussion, explain why you chose a particular solution.

- How did you create the user accounts? Did you use:
  - Active Directory Users and Computers?
  - A batch file and the **dsadd user** command?
  - A CSV file and import it by using the **csvde** command?
- How did you create the groups? Did you use:
  - Active Directory Users and Computers?
  - A batch file and the **dsadd group** command?
- How did you add members to the groups that you created? Did you use:
  - Active Directory Users and Computers?
  - A batch file and the **dsmod group** command?
- How did you resolve the following problems with the user accounts?
  - How did you enable Bjorn Rettig to logon?
  - Why was Mary Baker unable to logon to her computer?
  - Why was Bjorn Rettig unable to move Peter Houston's account to another organizational unit?

Best Practices for Managing Users

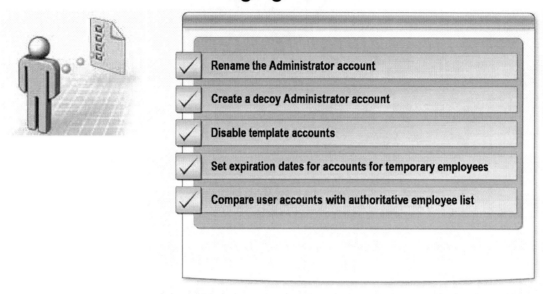

- Rename the Administrator account in each domain to reduce the risk of unauthorized use of this account.

- Create a decoy Administrator account.

  Create this new account with the name of "Administrator", remove all rights, make the user account a member of only the Domain Guests group, and then disable the account. When auditing of unsuccessful logon attempts is enabled, this decoy account simplifies auditing because an event will be added to the Event Log for each attack against the default Administrator account.

- Disable template accounts.

  Disabling templates prevents unauthorized users from using a template account to gain access to the network.

- Set expiration dates for accounts for short-term and temporary employees.

  Expiration dates will prevent temporary employees from accessing the network when their contracts expire. Ensure that human resources notify you when contracts are changed or extended.

- To find unauthorized or unused user accounts, compare the list domain user accounts with an authoritative list of employees, contractors, vendors, and authorized users provided by the human resources or payroll departments. Perform this task on a regular basis.

Best Practices for Managing Computers and Groups

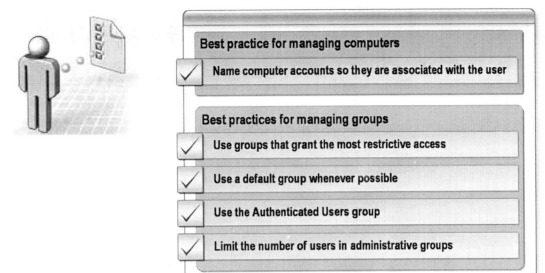

Best Practice for Managing Computers

- Name computer accounts so they are associated with the user.

  In environments where computers are not shared among multiple users, name computer accounts so they can be easily associated with the user. For example, the computer for the user kellyr could be named kellyr1. Adding a number after the computer name simplifies organization for users with multiple computers

Best Practices for Managing Groups

- Use groups that grant the most restrictive access.

  If you have multiple groups to which you can add user accounts, use the group that is most restrictive. However, ensure that you grant the appropriate user rights and permissions so that users can accomplish any required task.

- Use a default group whenever possible.

  Whenever a default group enables users to accomplish a task, use it instead of creating a new group. Create groups only when no default groups provide the required user rights and permissions.

- Use the Authenticated Users group instead of the Everyone group to grant most user rights and permissions.

  Using this group minimizes the risk of unauthorized access because Windows Server 2003 adds only valid user accounts to the Authenticated Users group.

- Limit the number of users in groups that have administrative privileges.

    Members of the Domain Admins, Enterprise Admins, Server Operators, Schema Admins, Administrators, Power Users, Print Operators, and Backup Operators groups have broad administrative privileges in a network environment. Add users to these groups only when the user will perform administrative tasks.

 Important Review current security-related best practices at www.microsoft.com/security.

Unit 3: Using the GPMC to Manage Group Policy

Contents

Overview	1
What Is the Group Policy Management Console?	3
Group Policy Modeling and Group Policy Results	4
Lab: Using the GPMC to Manage Group Policy	5
Lab Discussion	12
Best Practices	14

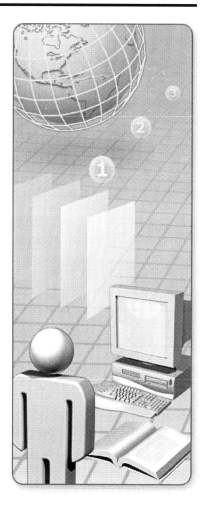

Information in this document, including URL and other Internet Web site references, is subject to change without notice. Unless otherwise noted, the example companies, organizations, products, domain names, e-mail addresses, logos, people, places, and events depicted herein are fictitious, and no association with any real company, organization, product, domain name, e-mail address, logo, person, place or event is intended or should be inferred. Complying with all applicable copyright laws is the responsibility of the user. Without limiting the rights under copyright, no part of this document may be reproduced, stored in or introduced into a retrieval system, or transmitted in any form or by any means (electronic, mechanical, photocopying, recording, or otherwise), or for any purpose, without the express written permission of Microsoft Corporation.

Microsoft may have patents, patent applications, trademarks, copyrights, or other intellectual property rights covering subject matter in this document. Except as expressly provided in any written license agreement from Microsoft, the furnishing of this document does not give you any license to these patents, trademarks, copyrights, or other intellectual property.

© 2003 Microsoft Corporation. All rights reserved.

Microsoft, MS-DOS, Windows, Windows NT, Windows Server 2003, Active Directory, MSDN, Windows Media, and Windows Server are either registered trademarks or trademarks of Microsoft Corporation in the United States and/or other countries.

The names of actual companies and products mentioned herein may be the trademarks of their respective owners.

Overview

- **What Is the Group Policy Management Console?**
- **Group Policy Modeling and Group Policy Results**
- **Lab: Using the GPMC to Manage Group Policy**
- **Lab Discussion**
- **Best Practices**

In conjunction with Microsoft® Windows Server™ 2003, Microsoft is releasing a new Group Policy management solution that unifies management of Group Policy. The Microsoft Group Policy Management Console (GPMC) provides a single solution for managing all Group Policy related tasks. It consists of a new Microsoft Management Console (MMC) snap-in and a set of scriptable interfaces for managing Group Policy. The GPMC helps you manage your enterprise more cost-effectively.

This unit will also introduce the following new Group Policy management features available in Windows Server 2003:

- Group Policy Modeling
- Group Policy Results

Objectives

After completing this learning unit, you will be able to:

- Implement Group Policy by using the GPMC, which includes:
    - Creating and linking a Group Policy object (GPO)
    - Linking and unlinking a GPO
    - Configuring Group Policy inheritance
    - Configuring security filtering for a GPO
    - Enabling or disabling a GPO
    - Deleting a GPO
    - Testing a GPO
- Manage GPOs by using the GPMC, which includes:
    - Editing the settings in a GPO
    - Backing up a GPO
    - Deleting a GPO
    - Copying a GPO
    - Importing a GPO
- Troubleshoot Group Policy, which includes:
    - Using Group Policy Results to troubleshoot Group Policy-related issues
    - Using Group Policy Modeling to experiment with possible Group Policy configurations

What Is the Group Policy Management Console?

The Group Policy Management Console (GPMC) is a new tool for managing Group Policy in Windows Server 2003.

The GPMC:

- Allows you to manage the Group Policy for multiple forests, domains, and organizational units from one consistent interface.
- Displays the linking, inheritance, and delegation of Group Policy
- Shows the container to which the policy applies.
- Provides an HTML report of the settings.
- Provides tools to show the Resultant Set of Policies (RSoP) and to experiment with proposed combinations of policies.

 Note The GPMC does not ship with Windows Server 2003. You can download it from http://www.microsoft.com/windowsserver2003/gpmc/default.mspx.

 Additional Information For more information about the GPMC, see the white paper *Administering Group Policy with Group Policy Management Console*, under Additional Reading on the Web page on the Student Materials compact disc.

Group Policy Modeling and Group Policy Results

Group Policy Modeling:
- Simulate a Group Policy deployment that would be applied to users and computers
- Requires a domain controller that is running Windows Server 2003 in the forest to simulate the policy deployment
- Simulate the resultant set of policy for any computer in the forest, including those running Windows 2000

Group Policy Results:
- Determine the resultant set of policy that was applied to a given computer and the user that logged on to that computer
- Determine the actual resultant set of policy data obtained from the target computer, not simulated data
- Cannot determine resultant set of policy data for computers running Windows 2000

Group Policy Modeling

Windows Server 2003 has a powerful new Group Policy management feature that allows the user to simulate a policy deployment that would be applied to users and computers before actually applying the policies. This feature, known as Resultant Set of Policy (RSoP) – Planning Mode in Windows Server 2003, is integrated into GPMC as Group Policy Modeling. This feature requires a domain controller that is running Windows Server 2003 in the forest because the simulation is performed by a service that is only present only on Windows Server 2003 domain controllers. However, by using this feature, you can simulate the resultant set of policy for any computer in the forest, including those running Microsoft Windows® 2000.

Group Policy Results

This feature allows administrators to determine the resultant set of policy that was applied to a specific computer and (optionally) the user that logged on to that computer. The data that is presented is similar to Group Policy Modeling data. However, unlike Group Policy Modeling, this data is not a simulation. It is the actual resultant set of policy data obtained from the target computer. Unlike Group Policy Modeling, the data from Group Policy Results is obtained from the client, and is not simulated on the domain controller. The client must be running Windows XP, Windows Server 2003, or later. It is not possible to get Group Policy Results data for a computer running Windows 2000 or earlier.

 Note Technically, a Windows Server 2003 domain controller is not required to access Group Policy Results. However, by default, only users with local administrator privileges on the target computer can remotely access Group Policy Results data. This can be delegated to additional users. However, the ability to delegate RSoP data is only available only in Active Directory forests that have the Windows Server 2003 schema in that forest.

Lab: Using the GPMC to Manage Group Policy

In this lab, you will:
- Implement a Group Policy scenario by using the GPMC
- Troubleshoot and resolve Group Policy issues by using the GPMC

After completing this lab, you will be able to:

- Implement a Group Policy scenario by using the GPMC.
- Troubleshoot and resolve Group Policy issues by using the GPMC.

Toolbox Resources

If necessary, use one or more of the following Toolbox resources to help you complete this lab:

- Linking, Disabling, and Deleting GPOs
- Exploring the GPMC
- Backing Up, Importing, and Restoring GPOs
- Copying and Pasting GPOs
- Blocking Inheritance and Enforcing a GPO
- Changing Apply and Deny Permissions
- Using Group Policy Results and Group Policy Modeling

Estimated time to complete this lab: **70 minutes**

Exercise 1
Implementing Group Policy by Using the GPMC

In this exercise, you will use the GPMC to implement a Group Policy solution.

Tasks	Supporting information
1. Remove any policies that are currently applied to the Sales organizational unit.	▪ Use the **Scope** tab to determine where a policy is linked. If a GPO is linked to any other organizational unit, remove the link without deleting the GPO. If the policy is not linked to anything else, you may safely delete it. See the Toolbox resource, Linking, Disabling, and Deleting GPOs.
2. Create a new GPO named **Desktop Restrictions** for the Sales organizational unit. The settings for **Desktop Restrictions** must meet the following requirements: • The **Shut Down** option on the **Start** menu must not be available. • The user's name must not be displayed on the **Start** menu. • The screen saver is password protected, but users may choose any screensaver. • The screen saver starts after 5 minutes of idle time. • Access to the registry editing tools is prevented. • Access to Task Manager is prevented.	All of the required settings are located under User Configuration, Administrative Templates. **Start Menu and Taskbar** ▪ Remove and prevent access to the **Shut Down** command (Enabled) ▪ Remove user name from **Start** menu (Enabled) **Control Panel/Display** ▪ Screen Saver (Enabled) ▪ Password protect the screen saver (Enabled) ▪ Screen Saver timeout (Enabled, 300 seconds) **System** ▪ Prevent access to registry editing tools (Enabled) **System/Ctrl+Alt+Del Options** ▪ Remove Task Manager (Enabled) See the Toolbox resource, Exploring the GPMC.

(continued)

Tasks	Supporting information
3. There is an existing GPO called **Default Logon Policy**. • Implement a similar policy for the Sales organizational unit and name it Sales Logon Policy. It should have the same settings except for Folder Redirection. • Redirect the My Documents folder to *\\ComputerName* SalesUsers (where *ComputerName* is your computer name). Create a new folder under this root for each user.	▪ To implement this requirement, you could: 　• Create a new GPO 　• Copy an existing GPO 　• Import from a backup up of a GPO ▪ Decide which approach is the best solution, and then implement it. You can use the space below to record your decision. Be prepared to explain your solution. _____ _____ _____ _____ See the following Toolbox resources: ▪ Backing Up, Importing, and Restoring GPOs ▪ Copying and Pasting GPOs

(continued)

Tasks	Supporting information
4. There is a global group called Sales IT, which contains members of all three sales organizational units. Configure Group Policy so that the members of Sales IT can use the registry editing tools from any computer. The remaining settings in the **Desktop Restrictions** GPO must still apply, and the **Sales Logon Policy** GPO must also apply.	■ To implement this requirement, you could: • Create a new organizational unit for the Sales IT users. Block inheritance of the **Desktop Restrictions** policy on the Sales IT organizational unit. Set the **Sales Logon** policy to **Enforced**. Create a new GPO that contains all of the settings from the **Desktop Restrictions** GPO, except the restriction on using the registry editing tools, and then link the new GPO to the new organizational unit. • Create a new GPO to allow access to the registry editing tools. Apply it to the Sales organizational unit. Change the security filtering to allow the policy to apply only to Sales IT. Change the link order of the new policy so it has the highest precedence. • Change the permissions of the GPO to deny application of the **Desktop Restrictions** policy to the Sales IT group. Create a new GPO that contains all of the settings from the **Desktop Restrictions** GPO except the restriction on using the registry editing tools. Set the permissions on the new GPO so that it only applies to the Sales IT group. ■ Decide which approach is the best solution, and then implement it. You can use the space below to record your decision. Be prepared to explain your solution. _____ _____ _____ _____ See the following Toolbox resources: ■ Blocking Inheritance and Enforcing a GPO ■ Changing Apply and Deny Permissions

(continued)

Tasks	Supporting information
5. Configure the users in the Sales Admin Assistants organizational unit so they do not have any of the desktop restrictions applied to them. But they should have the same logon policy settings as the other sales users.	▪ To implement this requirement, you could: • Block inheritance on the Sales Admin Assistants organizational unit, and then link the **Sales Logon Policy** to Sales Admin Assistants. • Create a new security group for the Sales Admin Assistants, and then change the permissions of the GPO to deny application of the policy to the new group. • Block inheritance on the Sales Admin Assistants organizational unit, and then set the **Sales Logon Policy** to be enforced. ▪ Decide which approach is the best solution, and then implement it. You can use the space below to record your decision. Be prepared to explain your solution. _____ _____ _____ _____ See the following Toolbox resources: ▪ Blocking Inheritance and Enforcing a GPO ▪ Changing Apply and Deny Permissions
6. Prepare a report showing what the effective Group Policy is for the following users: • kanel • koduris • barnhillj	▪ To implement this requirement, you could: • Create a report using the Group Policy Results Wizard. • Create a report using the Group Policy Modeling Wizard. ▪ Decide which approach is the best solution, and then implement it. You can use the space below to record your decision. Be prepared to explain your solution. _____ _____ _____ _____ See the Toolbox resource, Using Group Policy Results and Group Policy Modeling.

(*continued*)

Tasks	Supporting information
7. Verify the effective Group Policy for the following users: • kanel • koduris • barnhillj	▪ If you have successfully implemented Group Policy, the following conditions should be met: • kanel (Lori Kane's account is in the Sales organizational unit) will have the folder redirection, and all of the desktop restrictions applied. • koduris (Sunil Koduri is a member of the Sales IT global group) will have folder redirection and all of the desktop restrictions, except the registry tools restriction. • barnhillj (Josh Barnhill's user account is located in the Sales Admin Assistants organizational unit) will have no desktop restrictions, and will have the folder redirection applied.

Lab E-mail

From: Maria Hammond

To: Systems Administrators

Sent: Thu Sep 04 12:09:37 2003

Subject: New Group Policy settings

These are the Group Policy changes I'd like you to make on the Sales organizational unit. Under Sales, you'll have suborganizational units for the mobile sales force and for the sales administrative assistants. Here's what I'd like you to do:

1. Make sure there are no policies currently applied to the sales organizational unit. If there are any existing policies, either delete them or unlink them. Don't delete any policies that are currently linked to other organizational units.

2. Create a policy to configure desktop restrictions for everyone in the Sales organizational unit. They want the screen saver to have a password on it, and the screen saver should be set to start after 5 minutes of idle time. They do not want the user's name to appear on the Start Menu. Take away the Shut Down option on the Start Menu. It's also very important that you prevent access to the registry editing tools and to Task Manager.

3. There's a global group called Sales IT. Make sure they can still access the registry editing tools, regardless of the organizational unit where their account is located.

4. Every user in the Sales organization needs to have their My Documents folder redirected to a shared folder on the domain controller. Make sure that each user has their own folder below the shared folder, and that no user can access another user's folder.

Oh, I almost forgot - I don't want the sales administrative assistants to have the same desktop restrictions that I listed in #2. Is there some way you can prevent that without changing the organizational unit structure?

After you have implemented these Group Policy settings, please prepare a report showing what the effective group policy will be for some sample users.

I don't want a lot of angry sales users calling the help desk after you roll this out!

Maria Hammond, MCSE

Network Manager

NorthWind Traders, Inc.

Lab Discussion

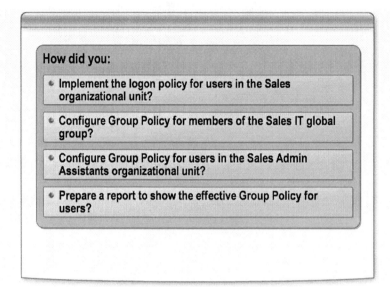

How did you:
- Implement the logon policy for users in the Sales organizational unit?
- Configure Group Policy for members of the Sales IT global group?
- Configure Group Policy for users in the Sales Admin Assistants organizational unit?
- Prepare a report to show the effective Group Policy for users?

Discuss with the class how you implemented the solutions in the preceding lab. During this discussion, explain why you chose a particular solution.

- How did you implement the logon policy for users in the Sales organizational unit? Did you:
  - Create a new GPO?
  - Copy an existing GPO?
  - Import from a backup of a GPO?
  - Use a different solution?
- How did you configure Group Policy so that members of the Sales IT security group could use the registry editing tools and access the command prompt from any computer? Did you:
  - Block inheritance on the Sales Admin Assistants organizational unit?
  - Create a new GPO on the same organizational unit that reverses the desktop restriction settings?
  - Create a new security group for the Sales Admin Assistants and change the permissions of the GPO to deny application of the policy to the new group?
  - Use a different solution?

- How did you configure Group Policy for users in the Sales Admin Assistants organizational unit so that they would not have any desktop restrictions applied to them, but would have the same logon script as the other sales users? Did you:
    - Block inheritance on the Sales Admin Assistants organizational unit?
    - Create a new GPO on the same organizational unit that reverses the desktop restriction settings?
    - Create a new security group for the Sales Admin Assistants and change the permissions of the GPO to deny application of the policy to the new group?
    - Use a different solution?
- How did you prepare a report to show the effective Group Policy for users Lori Kane, Sunil Koduri and Josh Barnhill? Did you:
    - Create a report using the Group Policy Results Wizard?
    - Create a report using the Group Policy Modeling Wizard?

Best Practices

- ✓ Determine where a GPO is linked before disabling
- ✓ Disable the unused portion of a GPO
- ✓ Determine where a GPO is linked before deleting
- ✓ Delete a GPO link that is not needed
- ✓ Limit the use of security filtering
- ✓ Test Group Policy before deploying to production
- ✓ Use the Settings tab to print a report of a tested GPO
- ✓ Limit the use of Block Inheritance and No Override

- Use the **Scope** tab to determine where a GPO is linked before disabling.

    If a GPO is linked to another container, do not disable the GPO. Disabling the GPO or a part of will affect the other container too.

- Disable the unused portion of a GPO.

    Each policy can contain computer and user settings. If you aren't using both in GPO, disable the unused portion to speed up processing.

- Use the **Scope** tab to determine where a GPO is linked before deleting.

    If a GPO is linked to another container, do not delete the GPO. Deleting the GPO might affect the other linked container too.

- Delete a GPO link rather than unlinking it.

    If you no longer need a policy, delete the GPO link rather than unlinking it to avoid confusion.

- Limit the use of security filtering.

    If you must use security filtering, filter on groups instead of individual users.

- Always test policies before deploying to the production environment.

    Testing policies before deploying will enable you to prevent the incorrect deployment of policies in your production environment.

- Use the **Settings** tab to print a report of a tested GPO.

    After you are satisfied with a policy, print a report of the tested GPO. The report will be useful during the policy deployment.

- Limit the use of Block Inheritance and No Override.

    Excessive use of Block Inheritance and No Override can complicate troubleshooting Group Policy problems.

Unit 4: Managing Resources and Security

Contents

Overview	1
Using Security Templates to Secure Your Network	2
Lab: Managing Resources and Security	4
Lab Discussion	9
Best Practices	10

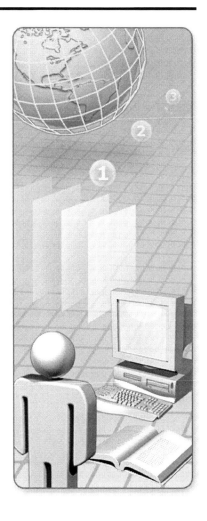

Information in this document, including URL and other Internet Web site references, is subject to change without notice. Unless otherwise noted, the example companies, organizations, products, domain names, e-mail addresses, logos, people, places, and events depicted herein are fictitious, and no association with any real company, organization, product, domain name, e-mail address, logo, person, place or event is intended or should be inferred. Complying with all applicable copyright laws is the responsibility of the user. Without limiting the rights under copyright, no part of this document may be reproduced, stored in or introduced into a retrieval system, or transmitted in any form or by any means (electronic, mechanical, photocopying, recording, or otherwise), or for any purpose, without the express written permission of Microsoft Corporation.

Microsoft may have patents, patent applications, trademarks, copyrights, or other intellectual property rights covering subject matter in this document. Except as expressly provided in any written license agreement from Microsoft, the furnishing of this document does not give you any license to these patents, trademarks, copyrights, or other intellectual property.

© 2003 Microsoft Corporation. All rights reserved.

Microsoft, MS-DOS, Windows, Windows NT, Windows Server 2003, Active Directory, MSDN, Windows Media, and Windows Server are either registered trademarks or trademarks of Microsoft Corporation in the United States and/or other countries.

The names of actual companies and products mentioned herein may be the trademarks of their respective owners.

Overview

- Using Security Templates to Secure Your Network
- Lab: Managing Resources and Security
- Lab Discussion
- Best Practices

As in Microsoft® Windows® 2000, using security templates and Group Policy to apply security settings to all computers in your enterprise is a security best practice in Windows Server™ 2003. This unit will review how to apply security settings by using security templates and Group Policy.

Additionally, Windows Server 2003 has two new capabilities for managing NTFS files and folders:

- *Effective permissions.* You can now display the effective permissions assigned to a specific user or group for any NTFS file or folder.

- *File or folder ownership.* A user or group with appropriate permissions can transfer the ownership of an NTFS file or folder to a specific user or group.

Objectives

After completing this unit, you will be able to:

- Create custom security templates.
- Configure NTFS permissions by using security templates.
- Apply security templates by using Group Policy.
- Audit security settings by using Security Configuration and Analysis.
- Determine the effective NTFS permissions for files and folders.
- Change the owner for an existing file or folder.

Using Security Templates to Secure Your Network

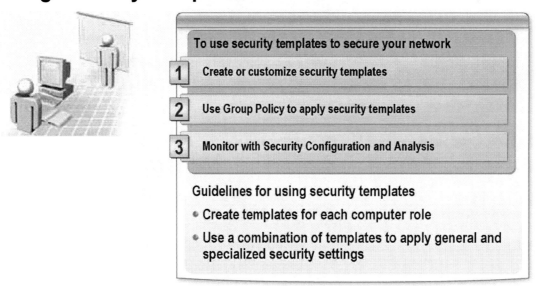

Security templates allow you to implement consistent, scalable, and reproducible security settings throughout your network. To use security templates to secure your network:

1. *Create or customize security templates.* You can use the sample templates located in the *systemroot*\Security\Templates folder with the Security Templates snap-in to create or modify templates.

2. *Use Group Policy to apply security templates.* After you have configured and tested security templates, use Group Policy to apply the security settings to computers throughout your enterprise. By using Group Policy you can automate the process of assigning templates, which allows you to standardize security settings by applying the same security template to multiple computers. Group Policy can also ensure that template settings are automatically reapplied to a computer if any security settings are changed locally.

3. *Monitor security settings by using Security Configuration and Analysis.* After deploying security settings, use the Security Configuration and Analysis snap-in on a regular basis to detect discrepancies between template settings and the current computer settings.

Guidelines for Using Security Templates

- *Use templates for each role.* The security settings for a specific computer role are usually the same for all computers that are assigned that role. For example, you can use one template for domain controllers and another template for client computers. Before you create templates, identify common computer roles, and then design a template for each role.

- *Use a combination of templates.* Often, some security settings must apply to all computers in an organization; and other security settings apply to only one type of computer role. For example, all computers in an organization may have a minimum password requirement for local computer accounts, but only Web servers require that IIS is running.

  To reduce complexity, create one template for all common settings, and then create another template for each specialized computer role. Apply the common template to all computers, and then apply the specialized template only to the computers that you created it for.

 Additional Information For more information about implementing security templates, see article 816297, "Define Security Templates By Using the Security Templates Snap-In in Windows Server 2003," in the Microsoft Knowledge Base at http://support.microsoft.com/?kbid=816297.

Lab: Managing Resources and Security

In this lab, you will:
- Configure security settings for multiple domain controllers
- Identify and resolve problems caused by overly restrictive security settings

After completing this lab, you will be able to:
- Configure security settings for multiple domain controllers.
- Identify and resolve problems caused by overly restrictive security settings.

Toolbox Resources

If necessary, use one or more of the following Toolbox resources to help you complete this lab:

- Using Security Configuration and Analysis to Determine and Configure Security Settings
- Default Auditing Settings in Windows Server 2003
- Pre-defined Security Templates in Windows Server 2003
- Creating Custom Security Templates
- Importing Security Templates into Group Policy
- Common Security Log Event IDs
- How to Verify the Effective Permissions on NTFS Files and Folders
- Changing the Owner for an Existing File or Folder

Estimated time to complete this lab: **45 minutes**

Exercise 1
Configuring Security Settings

In this exercise, you will create and apply a custom security template. You will also audit security settings and determine the effective permissions for a folder.

Tasks	Supporting information
1. Compare your current settings with the hisecdc template and note the differences.	See the following Toolbox resources: - Default Auditing Settings in Windows Server 2003 - Using Security Configuration and Analysis to Determine and Configure Security Settings - Pre-defined Security Templates in Windows Server 2003
2. Create a new template based on the hisecdc template, and make the following modifications: • The Print Spooler service and the Telnet service must be disabled on all domain controllers. • The permission on the C:\Reports folder on every domain controller must be set so that only Administrators have full control, DB Users have Read access, DB Operators have Modify access, and no other users have privileges.	See the Toolbox resource, Creating Custom Security Templates.

3. Apply the new security template for all domain controllers in your domain. Ensure that you apply the template so that the settings are automatically applied to new domain controllers.	- To apply the security template to all domain controllers, you could use:
	  • Group Policy
	  • Security Configuration and Analysis
	- Decide which approach is the best solution, and then implement it. You can use the space below to record your decision. Be prepared to explain your solution.
	
	_____
	_____
	_____
	_____
	
	See the Toolbox resource, Importing Security Templates into Group Policy.

(continued)

Tasks	Supporting information
4. Test to make sure that the auditing settings are working.	See the Toolbox resource, Common Security Log Event IDs.
5. Test to make sure that the DB users have only Read access and the DB operators have Modify access to the C:\Reports folder.	<ul><li>To verify the permissions, you could:<ul><li>View the access control list directly</li><li>Use effective permissions</li></ul></li><li>Decide which approach is the best solution, and then implement it. You can use the space below to record your decision. Be prepared to explain your solution.</li></ul> _____ _____ _____ _____ See the Toolbox resource, How to Verify the Effective Permissions on NTFS Files and Folders.

Exercise 2
Troubleshooting Security Settings

In this exercise, you will resolve the problems described below. For each problem, identify the cause and correct the issue.

Issues	Supporting information
1. John Frum has recently taken over responsibility for managing the logs, but he can't access a file in the C:\Logs folder. Make John the owner of the C:\Logs folder so that he can access the files.	▪ For a hint, see the Toolbox resource, Troubleshooting Security Settings. See the Toolbox resource, Changing the Owner for an Existing File or Folder.
2. You need to modify a file in the *ComputerName*\ Daily Reports (where *ComputerName* is the name of your computer) shared folder, but you are denied access. Diagnose and fix the problem. Be prepared to describe the tools you used to identify the cause of the problem.	▪ For a hint, see the Toolbox resource, Troubleshooting Security Settings.
3. Holly Holt was unable to log onto the computer BLUEK1. Use the Security event log named Security-event-log.evt in the Network Files folder to diagnose the source of the problem. Do not fix the problem.	▪ For a hint, see the Toolbox resource, Troubleshooting Security Settings. See the Toolbox resource, Common Security Log Event IDs.

Lab E-mail

From: Maria Hammond

To: Systems Administrators

Sent: Thu Sep 04 12:20:37 2003

Subject: Resource security

Our company security policy states that all domain controllers must be using the hisecdc template with the following additions:

- The print spooler service and the Telnet service must be disabled on all domain controllers.
- The permission on the C:\Reports folder on every domain controller must be set so that only Administrators have full control, DB Users have Read access, DB Operators have Modify access, and no other users have privileges.

Please compare your current settings against the hisecdc template and be prepared to tell me the differences. Bring your server up to the required specifications immediately. The security team will be auditing the other domain controllers in your domain, so be prepared to bring those controllers up to specifications as well. You should set it up so that future domain controllers will meet these requirements, too.

Make sure you test everything.

Maria Hammond, MCSE

Network Manager

NorthWind Traders, Inc.

Lab Discussion

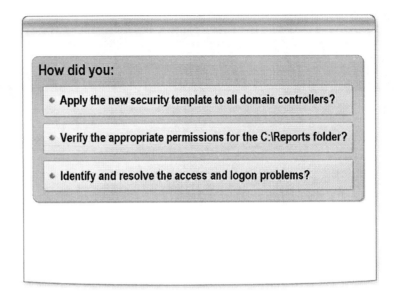

Discuss with the class how you implemented the solutions in the preceding lab. During this discussion, explain why you chose a particular solution.

- How did you apply the new security template to all domain controllers in your domain? Did you use:
  - Group Policy?
  - Security Configuration and Analysis?
- How did you verify that the DB Users and DB Operators groups had the appropriate permissions for the C:\Reports folder? Did you:
  - View the discretionary access control lists directly?
  - Use the Effective Permissions tool?
- How did you resolve the following access and logon problems:
  - Why was John Frum unable to access the C:\Logs folder?
  - Why were you unable to modify a file in the Daily Reports shared folder?
  - Why was Holly Holt unable to log onto the domain controller?

Best Practices

Best Practices for Using Security Templates

- Always test security templates before applying them to your network.

    Do not apply predefined or newly-created security templates to your computer or network without testing to ensure that the right level of application functionality is maintained.

- Never edit the Setup Security.inf template because it gives you the option to reapply the default security settings.

    If you ever remove a security template from a Group Policy object (GPO), appropriately reapply the Setup Security.inf to restore all default settings. The Setup Security.inf template should be applied only to the local computer by using **secedit** or Security Configuration and Analysis. It is preferable to apply it to parts of a GPO by using the **Secedit** command-line tool.

- Do not modify predefined templates.

    Instead of modifying a predefined template, customize the predefined template and then save the changes with a different template name. Because these templates were designed for specific needs, having the original template will always give you the option of using it.

- Choose the appropriate default level of computer access.

    When deciding on the default level of computer access for users, the determining factor is the installed base of applications that must be supported. For example, if users use only applications that belong to the Windows Logo Program for Software, then you can make all users members of the Users group. If not, you may have to add users to the Power Users group so that they have the appropriate privileges to use the application, which is less secure.

Best Practices for Using Security Configuration and Analysis

- Use Security Configuration and Analysis only to configure security areas not affected by Group Policy settings.

  This includes areas such as security on local files and folders, registry keys, and system services. Otherwise, Group Policy settings will override the local settings.

- In environments that do not use Active Directory, use the **secedit** command line tool to automate security analysis and configuration tasks in a large enterprise.

  By using Secedit.exe from a command prompt, from a batch file, or by using a task scheduler, you can automatically create and apply templates, and analyze system security on multiple computers.

- In environments that use Active Directory, use Group Policy rather than Security Configuration and Analysis when you are configuring security for a large number of computers.

  If you use Security Configuration and Analysis, you must configure each client computer individually. Instead, create a security template, and then import it to a GPO so that Group Policy applies it to computers in your enterprise.

Unit 5: Managing DNS

Contents

Overview	1
What Are DNS Stub Zones?	3
What Is Conditional Forwarding?	4
Lab: Installing and Configuring DNS	6
Lab Discussion	12
Best Practices	13

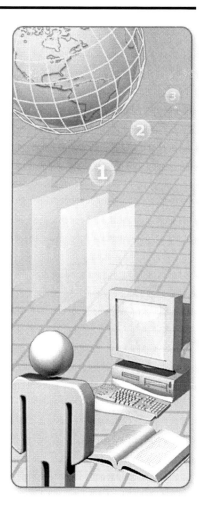

Information in this document, including URL and other Internet Web site references, is subject to change without notice. Unless otherwise noted, the example companies, organizations, products, domain names, e-mail addresses, logos, people, places, and events depicted herein are fictitious, and no association with any real company, organization, product, domain name, e-mail address, logo, person, place or event is intended or should be inferred. Complying with all applicable copyright laws is the responsibility of the user. Without limiting the rights under copyright, no part of this document may be reproduced, stored in or introduced into a retrieval system, or transmitted in any form or by any means (electronic, mechanical, photocopying, recording, or otherwise), or for any purpose, without the express written permission of Microsoft Corporation.

Microsoft may have patents, patent applications, trademarks, copyrights, or other intellectual property rights covering subject matter in this document. Except as expressly provided in any written license agreement from Microsoft, the furnishing of this document does not give you any license to these patents, trademarks, copyrights, or other intellectual property.

© 2003 Microsoft Corporation. All rights reserved.

Microsoft, MS-DOS, Windows, Windows NT, Windows Server 2003, Active Directory, MSDN, Windows Media, and Windows Server are either registered trademarks or trademarks of Microsoft Corporation in the United States and/or other countries.

The names of actual companies and products mentioned herein may be the trademarks of their respective owners.

Overview

- What Are DNS Stub Zones?
- What Is Conditional Forwarding?
- Lab: Installing and Configuring DNS
- Lab Discussion
- Best Practices

The Domain Name System (DNS) is an integral part of client/server communications in Internet Protocol (IP) networks. DNS is a distributed database that is used in IP networks to translate, or resolve, computer names into IP addresses. Clients use the DNS Server service for name resolution and to locate services, including domain controllers that provide user authentication.

There are some significant improvements in name resolution in Microsoft® Windows Server™ 2003 DNS over Windows® 2000 DNS. The new features in Windows Server 2003 DNS that make DNS administration easier include:

- DNS stub zones
- Conditional forwarding

Additionally, Windows Server 2003 also provides the DNS administrative tool to perform common administrative tasks.

Objectives

After completing this learning unit, you will be able to:

- Install DNS by using the Manage Your Server tool.
- Create forward lookup zones.
- Create reverse lookup zones.
- Configure DNS conditional forwarding.
- Configure DNS zones, which includes:
    - Configuring zone options.
    - Configuring zones for secure dynamic update.
    - Configuring Active Directory integrated zones.
- Create DNS stub zones.

 Additional Information For more information about DNS, see the multimedia presentation *The Role of DNS in the Network Infrastructure*, under Multimedia on the Web page on the Student Materials compact disc. After you open the multimedia presentation, press F11 to view it in full-screen mode.

What Are DNS Stub Zones?

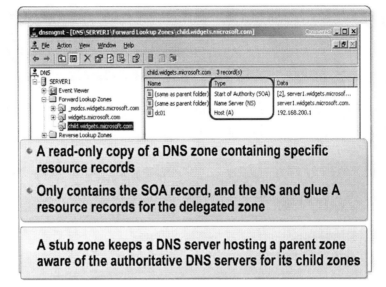

- A read-only copy of a DNS zone containing specific resource records
- Only contains the SOA record, and the NS and glue A resource records for the delegated zone

A stub zone keeps a DNS server hosting a parent zone aware of the authoritative DNS servers for its child zones

---

A *stub zone* is:

- A read-only copy of a DNS zone that contains only the resource records necessary to identify the authoritative DNS servers for the actual zone.
- Like a secondary zone, except that it replicates only the necessary records of a master zone instead of the entire zone. The stub zone contains only the:
  - SOA (start of authority) resource record.
  - Name Server (NS) resource records.
  - Glue host (A) resource records.

 Note The administrator cannot modify a stub zone's resource records. Any changes that the administrator wants to make to the resource records in a stub zone must be made in the original primary zone from which the stub zone is derived.

A stub zone is used to keeps a DNS server hosting a parent zone aware of the authoritative DNS servers for its child zone and, thereby, maintain DNS name resolution efficiency.

 Additional Information For more information about DNS stub zones, see the Support WebCast, "*Microsoft Windows Server 2003 DNS: Stub Zones and Conditional Forwarding*" at http://support.microsoft.com/default.aspx?scid=/servicedesks/webcasts/wc012103/wcblurb012103.asp.

What Is Conditional Forwarding?

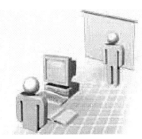
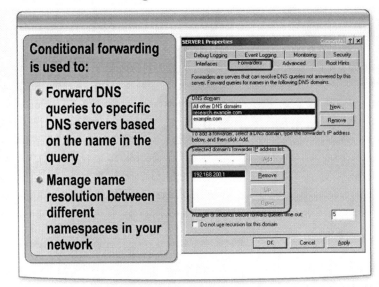

Conditional forwarding is used to:
- Forward DNS queries to specific DNS servers based on the name in the query
- Manage name resolution between different namespaces in your network

---

A *forwarder* is a designated DNS server that forwards queries for resolving external domain names. Forwarders reduce the amount of name resolution traffic across the wide area network (WAN.)

Conditional forwarding is used to:

- Forward DNS queries to specific DNS servers based on the DNS domain names in the queries.

    For example, by using conditional forwarding, all queries to a DNS server for names ending with nwtraders.msft can be forwarded to a specific DNS server's IP address, or to the IP addresses of multiple DNS servers.

- Manage name resolution between different namespaces in your network.

    For example, when two companies (nwtraders.msft and contoso.msft) merge or collaborate, they may want to allow clients from the internal namespace of one company to resolve the names of the clients from the internal namespace of another company.

    The administrators at nwtraders.msft may inform the administrators of contoso.msft about the set of DNS servers that they can use for name resolution within nwtraders.msft. In this case, the DNS servers within contoso.msft will be configured to forward all queries for names ending with nwtraders.msft to the designated DNS servers.

 Note An authoritative DNS server cannot forward queries based on domain names for which it is authoritative. The authoritative DNS server must respond to these queries, and not forward them.

For example, the authoritative DNS server for the zone na.nwtraders.msft cannot forward queries based on the domain name na.nwtraders.msft. If the DNS server were allowed to do this, it would nullify the server's ability to respond to queries for the domain name na.nwtraders.msft. The authoritative DNS server for na.nwtraders.msft can forward queries for DNS names that end with sales.na.nwtraders.msft, if sales.na.nwtraders.msft is delegated to another DNS server.

How Does Conditional Forwarding Work

A conditional forwarder setting consists of a domain name and the IP addresses of one or more forwarders. To configure a DNS server for conditional forwarding, set up a list of domain names and IP addresses on the DNS server.

When a DNS client or server performs a query operation against a DNS server configured for forwarding, the following tasks are performed:

1. First the DNS server looks to see if the query can be resolved by using its own zone data.

2. If the query cannot be resolved by using the zone data, the DNS server checks its cache.

3. If the query cannot be resolved by using the cache, the DNS server uses the forwarders list to resolve the query.

   If the DNS server is configured to forward for the domain name designated in the query (a match), the query is forwarded to the IP address of a forwarder associated with the domain name.

4. If the DNS server has no domain name listed for the name designated in the query, it attempts to resolve the query by using standard recursion.

Tip You can disable recursion specifically for each forwarder.

Additional Information For more information about conditional forwarding, see the Support WebCast, "*Microsoft Windows Server 2003 DNS: Stub Zones and Conditional Forwarding*" at http://support.microsoft.com/default.aspx?scid=/servicedesks/webcasts/wc012103/wcblurb012103.asp.

Lab: Installing and Configuring DNS

In this lab, you will:
- Install DNS by using the Manage Your Server tool
- Configure DNS

After completing this lab, you will be able to:

- Install DNS by using the Manage Your Server tool.
- Configure DNS.

Toolbox Resources

If necessary, use one or more of the following Toolbox resources to help you complete this lab:

- Using Manage Your Server to Install and Configure DNS
- DNS Name Resolution Methods
- Configuring Conditional Forwarding
- Delegating a Subdomain and Creating Stub Zones
- Configuring the SOA Record for a DNS Zone
- Configuring Active Directory Integrated Zones
- Configuring Secure Dynamic Updates

Estimated time to complete this lab: **60 minutes**

Exercise 1
Installing and Configuring DNS

In this exercise, you will install and configure DNS.

Tasks	Supporting information
1. Install and configure DNS. • Create a standard primary forward lookup zone for your domain (do not store the zone in Active Directory). • Create a standard secondary reverse lookup zone for your network (do not store the zone in Active Directory). • Enable nonsecure and secure dynamic updates for both zones. Do not enable forwarders at this time. • Use the london.nwtraders.msft DNS server as the master for the zone.	▪ Ensure that operating system components are installed according to company policy. ▪ Remember to change the properties of your Local Area Connection to use your own DNS Server for name resolution. **Note:** The primary forward lookup zone will be converted to an Active Directory integrated zone later in this lab. See the Toolbox resource, Using Manage Your Server to Install and Configure DNS.
2. Notify the corporate DNS administrator that you have completed setting up your zones. The corporate DNS administrator will delete your old zone from the corporate DNS server.	

Unit 5: Managing DNS

(*continued*)

Tasks	Supporting information
3. After all of the subsidiary zones have been created, and the old zones deleted from the corporate DNS server, configure your DNS server so that it can resolve all of the domains in the Northwind Traders enterprise. Use nslookup to verify that name resolution is functioning correctly.	■ To implement this requirement, you could: • Add secondary forward lookup zones to your DNS server for each of the subsidiary zones. • Use conditional forwarding to forward queries for each of the subsidiary zones to the correct DNS server. ■ Decide which approach is the best solution, and then implement it. You can use the space below to record your decision. Be prepared to explain your solution. **Note:** Be sure to refer to the e-mail message from Maria before choosing an option. See the following Toolbox resources: ■ DNS Name Resolution Methods ■ Configuring Conditional Forwarding
4. To prepare for the addition of a new child domain to your existing domain, delegate a new subdomain, called development, to the corporate DNS server. Remember that the corporate DNS administrator may add or remove name servers from the delegated subdomain. Notify the corporate DNS administrator when you have completed the delegation.	■ To implement this requirement, you could: • Delegate the new subdomain. If a name server is added or removed, update the delegation manually on your server. • Delegate the new subdomain. Create a stub zone on your DNS server for the delegated subdomain. ■ Decide which approach is the best solution, and then implement it. You can use the space below to record your decision. Be prepared to explain your solution. See the Toolbox resource, Delegating a Subdomain and Creating Stub Zones.
5. Configure the Time to Live (TTL) value for the Start of Authority (SOA) record for your zone to be 6 hours. All other records in the zone must have a TTL value of 3 hours.	■ The TTL value of a record is used to determine how long DNS servers, and some DNS clients, are allowed to cache information about the record. See the Toolbox resource, Configuring the SOA Record for a DNS Zone.

(*continued*)

Tasks	Supporting information
6. Configure the primary zone on your DNS server so that it is stored in Active Directory.	▪ Zone files can either be stored in text files, or in Active Directory. Storing a zone file in Active Directory provides greater security, and enables the transfer of zone information to be managed by Active Directory replication. See the Toolbox resource, Configuring Active Directory Integrated Zones.
7. Configure your primary zone to accept only secure dynamic updates.	▪ Enabling secure dynamic updates allows you to use standard Windows security features to control which computers can update records in an Active Directory integrated zone. See the Toolbox resource, Configuring Secure Dynamic Updates.

Lab E-mail

From: Maria Hammond

To: Systems Administrators

Sent: Thu Sep 04 12:37:46 2003

Subject: FWD: DNS restructuring

Here's the e-mail on the DNS configuration requirements from the design team. If you have any questions, please ask me and I will forward it to them.

Thanks,

Maria

-----Original Message-----

From: Infrastructure Design Team

To: Subsidiary Network Managers

Subject: DNS restructuring

The DNS server in corporate headquarters is becoming overloaded and a decision has been made to install and configure DNS servers in each of the subsidiary offices.

Each subsidiary office will be responsible for creating a standard primary forward lookup zone to support their Active Directory directory service domain, as well a creating a standard secondary reverse lookup zone using the corporate headquarters DNS server as the master server for the zone.

After you have completed the installation and configuration of DNS in your subsidiary, you must notify the DNS administrator at corporate headquarters so that the existing primary forward lookup zone for you domain can be removed from the corporate DNS server.

You must also ensure that you are able to resolve host names in all of the other subsidiary offices, as well as in corporate headquarters. The DNS design team has determined that using secondary lookup zones will generate too much network traffic, so using secondary lookup zones to accomplish this task is not an option.

The Active Directory Design team has determined that all subsidiary offices will require an additional child domain at some point in the future. As part of the DNS restructuring, you are required to delegate a subdomain to the corporate DNS server that will be used for the additional child domain in the future. The new child domain is named Development. Keep in mind that the DNS administrator will be adding and removing name servers for the delegated domain, and that your DNS server must be updated automatically whenever a NS record is changed in the delegated subdomain.

Finally, you must make sure that the following tasks are completed:

- The TTL value for the SOA record for all primary forward lookup zones must be set to 6 hours. The TTL for all other resource records must be set to 3 hours.
- Dynamic updates must be enabled; however, only secure dynamic updates are permitted.
- All primary forward lookup zones must be stored in Active Directory.

Lab Discussion

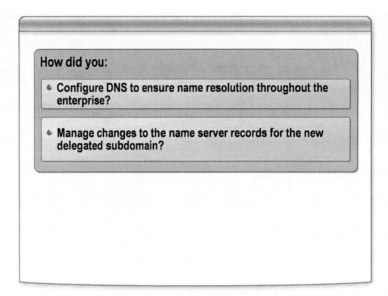

Discuss with the class how you implemented the solutions in the preceding lab. During this discussion, explain why you chose a particular solution.

- After creating a new primary forward lookup zone for your domain, how did you configure DNS to ensure that name resolution functioned throughout the enterprise? Did you:
  - Create secondary forward lookup zones on your DNS server for each of the subsidiary domains?
  - Use conditional forwarding?
- After delegating the new subdomain to the corporate DNS server, how did you manage changes to the name server records for the delegated subdomain? Did you:
  - Update the delegation manually on your server?
  - Create a stub zone on your DNS server for the delegated subdomain?

Best Practices

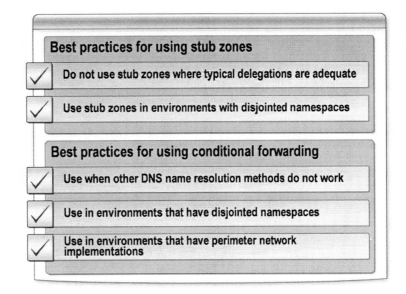

Best Practices for Using Stub Zones

- Do not use stub zones in a configuration in which typical delegations are adequate.

    Using both stub zones and delegations can cause confusion administering the DNS server. The DNS server will use a stub zone first and ignore the delegation.

- Use stub zones when the problem cannot be solved by using delegation, such as in environments containing disjointed namespaces.

    Typically, environments containing contiguous namespaces will not benefit using stub zones.

 Note The primary restriction for a stub zone is that it can not be hosted on a DNS server that is authoritative for the same zone.

Best Practices for Using Conditional Forwarding

- Use conditional forwarding when the problem cannot be solved by using a shared root, secondary zones, or standard forwarding.

- Use conditional forwarding in environments that contain disjointed namespaces.

    Environments containing contiguous namespaces will not benefit from using conditional forwarding.

- Use conditional forwarding in environments that have namespace issues caused by perimeter network implementations.

    Namespace issues in environments with perimeter network implementations cannot be solved by using a shared root, secondary zones, or standard forwarding.

 Additional Information For more information about using stub zones and conditional forwarding, see Appendix B, "DNS Name Resolution Methods" in Workshop 2209, *Expert Track: Updating Systems Administrator Skills from Microsoft Windows 2000 to Windows Server 2003*.

Unit 6: Managing Servers

Contents

Overview	1
What is Remote Desktop for Administration?	2
Lab: Managing Servers	4
Lab E-mail	7
Lab Discussion	8
Best Practices	9

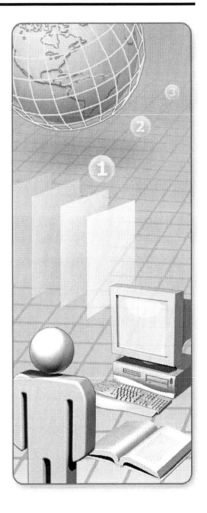

Information in this document, including URL and other Internet Web site references, is subject to change without notice. Unless otherwise noted, the example companies, organizations, products, domain names, e-mail addresses, logos, people, places, and events depicted herein are fictitious, and no association with any real company, organization, product, domain name, e-mail address, logo, person, place or event is intended or should be inferred. Complying with all applicable copyright laws is the responsibility of the user. Without limiting the rights under copyright, no part of this document may be reproduced, stored in or introduced into a retrieval system, or transmitted in any form or by any means (electronic, mechanical, photocopying, recording, or otherwise), or for any purpose, without the express written permission of Microsoft Corporation.

Microsoft may have patents, patent applications, trademarks, copyrights, or other intellectual property rights covering subject matter in this document. Except as expressly provided in any written license agreement from Microsoft, the furnishing of this document does not give you any license to these patents, trademarks, copyrights, or other intellectual property.

© 2003 Microsoft Corporation. All rights reserved.

Microsoft, MS-DOS, Windows, Windows NT, Windows Server 2003, Active Directory, MSDN, Windows Media, and Windows Server are either registered trademarks or trademarks of Microsoft Corporation in the United States and/or other countries.

The names of actual companies and products mentioned herein may be the trademarks of their respective owners.

Overview

- **What is Remote Desktop for Administration?**
- **Lab: Managing Servers**
- **Lab Discussion**
- **Best Practices**

Microsoft® Windows Server™ 2003 provides many tools for managing computers. In particular, there are new remote administration tools that enable you to administer servers from any computer on your network. By using these remote administration tools, you can access Microsoft Management Console (MMC) snap-ins, such as Active Directory Users and Computers, Control Panel, and most other administrative tools on a remote computer. Additionally, you can configure MMC snap-ins to perform similar tasks on multiple servers.

Objectives

After completing this unit, you will be able to:

- Describe the components and functions of Remote Desktop for Administration.
- Determine the best tool to use for remote administration in specific situations.
- Create desktop shortcuts that run the **runas** command.
- Connect to a remote server by using the Remote Desktops snap-in.
- Connect to a remote server by using Remote Desktop Connection.
- Configure Remote Desktop Connection.

 Additional Information For more information about the best administration tool to use in a specific situation, see "Remote administration overview" in Windows Server 2003 Help and Support.

What is Remote Desktop for Administration?

- **Remote Desktop for Administration is a tool suite used to connect to and administer computers remotely**
    - Uses the Remote Desktop Protocol
    - Provides two remote connections to a computer
    - Is disabled by default in Windows Server 2003
    - Includes the Remote Desktop Users group
- **Remote Desktop clients include:**
    - Remote Desktop Connection—Use to connect to one computer
    - Remote Desktops MMC snap-in—Use to create connections to multiple computers
- **Use mstsc.exe /console to use Remote Desktop Connection to connect to the console session of a remote computer**

Remote Desktop for Administration (formerly known as Terminal Services in Remote Administration mode in Windows 2000) provides you with the ability to remotely access computers on your network. Through a Terminal Services session, you can access MMC snap-ins, such as Active Directory Users and Computers, Control Panel, and most other administrative tools on a remote computer. This capability allows you to administer servers from any computer on your network.

Remote Desktop for Administration:

- Uses the Remote Desktop Protocol (RDP), which transmits the user interface to the client session, and transmits the keyboard and mouse clicks from the client to the server.

- Provides two simultaneous Remote Desktop connections (in addition to the server console session) by default. To allow more than two remote connections, you must install Terminal Services.

- Is disabled by default in Windows Server 2003. You must log on locally to enable Remote Desktop connections.

- Includes the Remote Desktop Users group, which is a default local group in Windows Server 2003. Members of this group are granted the right to logon remotely.

Remote Desktop Clients

Remote Desktop for Administration provides the following two GUI-based RDP clients that you can use to log on to a remote computer and perform administrative tasks as if you were sitting at the console:

- *Remote Desktop Connection.* Use to log on to one computer remotely. You can configure settings for the connection, and then save the settings for the next time you connect.

- *Remote Desktops MMC snap-in.* Use to create remote connections to multiple computers. By using the console tree, you can switch among connections to several remote computers. By default, the Remote Desktops snap-in connects you to the console session of a remote computer.

The Mstsc.exe Command

Mstsc.exe is the command line command for the Remote Desktop Connection GUI-based client. The advantage of using the Mstsc.exe command is the ability to run Remote Desktop Connection with additional options. For example, to connect to the console session of a computer by using Remote Desktop Connection, use the following command:

mstsc.exe /console

To view all of the options for the Mstce.exe command, at a command prompt, type **mstsc /?**

 Important Remote Desktop for Administration allows you to either start a new remote session on a server or to remotely connect to the console session. However, there can be only one console session running on a server at one time. If you log on to the console session remotely while another administrator is sitting at the console, that administrator is locked out.

Lab: Managing Servers

In this lab, you will:
- Determine the appropriate tool to use for remote administration
- Manage servers remotely by using alternate credentials
- Troubleshoot and resolve problems with Remote Desktop connections

After completing this lab, you will be able to:

- Determine the appropriate tool to use for remote administration.
- Manage servers remotely by using alternate credentials.
- Troubleshoot and resolve problems with Remote Desktop connections.

Toolbox Resources

If necessary, use one or more of the following Toolbox resources to help you complete this lab:

- Creating Custom Shortcuts with the **Runas** Command
- Using the Remote Desktops MMC
- Using the Remote Desktop Connection
- Using the Command Line RDP client
- Viewing Device Driver Details
- Setting Up Remote Desktop for Administration
- The Differences Between Logging Off and Disconnecting From a Remote Desktop Session
- Configuring Client Connection Speed and Configuring Auto Reconnect
- Accessing a Remote Desktop Connection by Using a Smart Card Logon

Estimated time to complete this lab: **45 minutes**

Exercise 1
Managing Servers Remotely

In this exercise, you will create customized MMC consoles and create and use shortcuts that run the **Runas** command. You will also use Remote Desktop for Administration tools.

Tasks	Supporting information
1. Create shortcuts that will let you access Active Directory Users and Computers, Computer Management, and run a command prompt with administrative rights.	<ul><li>To implement this requirement, you could:<ul><li>Create a custom MMC with all snap-ins, and use the **Run As** shortcut option; create a separate shortcut for the command prompt.</li><li>Create separate shortcuts for each console by using the **Runas** command.</li></ul></li><li>Decide which approach is the best solution, and then implement it. You can use the space below to record your decision. Be prepared to explain your solution.</li></ul> _____ _____ _____ See the Toolbox resource, Create Custom Shortcuts with the RunAs Command.
2. Configure your server so administrators can connect remotely.	See the Toolbox resource, Setting Up Remote Desktop for Administration.
3. Write down the driver details for the mouse device driver on Glasgow. Use the account *Contoso\Administrator* to access Glasgow.	<ul><li>To implement this requirement, you could:<ul><li>Connect to Glasgow by using Computer Management.</li><li>Connect by using the Remote Desktops MMC, the Remote Desktop Connection tool, or the **Mstsc** command, and then run an administrative tool on the remote system.</li></ul></li><li>Decide which approach is the best solution, and then implement it. You can use the space below to record your decision. Be prepared to explain your solution.</li></ul> _____ _____ _____ See the following Toolbox resources:<ul><li>Using the Remote Desktops MMC</li><li>Using the Remote Desktop Connection</li><li>Using the Command Line RDP Client</li><li>Viewing Device Driver Details</li><li>The Differences Between Logging Off and Disconnecting From a Remote Desktop Session</li></ul>

Exercise 2
Troubleshooting Remote Desktop Connections

In this exercise, you will identify the cause and resolve the problem described below.

Issues	Supporting information
1. You have had problems with the connection speed when using remote desktop connection from home on your 28.8K modem. Because of line noise, you often lose your connection.	▪ For a hint, see the Toolbox resource, Troubleshooting Remote Desktop Connections. See the Toolbox resource, Configuring Client Connection Speed and Configuring Auto Reconnect.

Lab E-mail

From: Maria Hammond

To: Systems Administrators

Sent: Thu Sep 04 13:08:30 2003

Subject: Setting up short cuts

If you haven't set up your shortcuts yet, please make sure you have RunAs shortcuts to Active Directory Users and Computers, Computer Management, and a command prompt. That way you're less likely to forget about the principle of least privilege.

I need to know the details for the mouse driver we're using on Glasgow. Please write down the file names and versions. You can access Glasgow by using the Contoso\Administrator account with the company standard admin password.

Oh, one more thing. Please make sure your server is enabled for remote administration. Josh Barnhill needs access to it and he couldn't get to it the other day. He's been approved to access it remotely for some Sales IT tasks.

Thanks!

Maria Hammond, MCSE

Network Manager

NorthWind Traders, Inc.

Lab Discussion

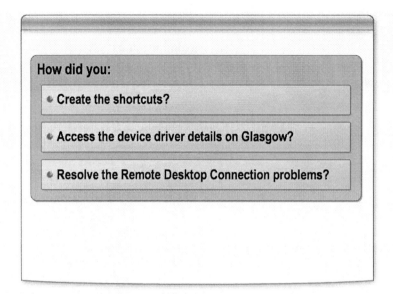

Discuss with the class how you implemented the solutions in the preceding lab. During this discussion, explain why you chose a particular solution.

- How did you create the shortcuts to access Active Directory Users and Computers and Device Manager, and to start a command prompt with administrative privileges? Did you:
  - Create a customized MMC console with the appropriate snap-ins and a Run As shortcut for the command prompt?
  - Create a separate shortcut for each snap-in by using the **runas** command?
- How did you access the details for the mouse device driver on Glasgow? Did you:
  - Connect by using Computer Management?
  - Connect by using Remote Desktop Connection and run the administrative tool on Glasgow?
- How did you resolve the following Remote Desktop Connection problems:
  - How did you address the connection speed issue when using Remote Desktop Connection from home?
  - Why were you unable to log onto a remote computer using a smartcard?

Best Practices

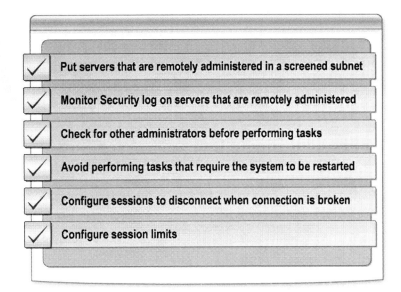

- Put servers that are remotely administered in a screened subnet.

    Because of the security implications of remote logons, any user who logs on remotely (as well as from the Internet) can perform tasks as though they were sitting at the console. For this reason, ensure that a firewall separates the server from the internal network.

- Monitor the Security log on servers that are remotely administered.

    If a remotely administered server is compromised, the attacker can use the remote administration capabilities as a launching point for attacks against other systems. Closely monitoring the Security log in Event Viewer will reveal audit events that indicate a successful logon by an attacker.

- Check for the presence of other administrators before performing tasks on a remoter server.

    Use the Terminal Services Manager tool or the **query user** command line utility to check for the presence of other administrators. Although the two default remote connection allows flexibility to administer servers, this capability is not designed to support multiple simultaneous administrators. Administrators need to ensure that they do not perform potentially destructive operations at the same time. For example, two administrators trying to reconfigure the disk subsystem can undermine each other's work, or even worse, destroy data.

- Avoid performing tasks on remote servers that require that the system be restarted.

    Some tasks, for example system upgrades and domain controller promotion, require that the system be restarted at their completion. These tasks work correctly from within a Remote Desktop session, but something as simple as a floppy disk in the drive or a bad boot sector on the disk could prevent the server from restarting. Therefore, do not remotely restart mission-critical servers unless you have the ability to physically intervene at the server if a problem occurs.

- Configure Remote Desktop sessions to disconnect when the connection to the remote computer is broken.

    If a session is interrupted due to a network problem, the session goes into a disconnected state and continues executing the processes that were running before the interruption occurred. If the session is configured to reset when the connection breaks, all processes running in that session will stop; this is similar to stopping an application by using End Task.

- Configure session limits.

    Because it is not possible to have more than two remote sessions, remote administrators might be locked out of a server if two remote sessions are in either an active or disconnected state. To prevent this from happening, configure the duration after which the session will be reset. When configuring this property, it is critical that sessions that are disconnected do not get reset prematurely. For this reason, it may be useful to perform remote administration tasks that should not be accidentally reset using a shared administrator account, such as a local machine account. Use the account **Properties** tab to configure this user account not to reset after it is disconnected.

 Additional Information To perform this task, see "To change settings for when a session limit is reached or connection is broken," in Windows Server 2003 Help and Support.

Unit 7: Managing Terminal Services

Contents

Overview	1
Terminal Server Licensing	2
Lab: Managing Terminal Services	4
Lab Discussion	8
Best Practices	9

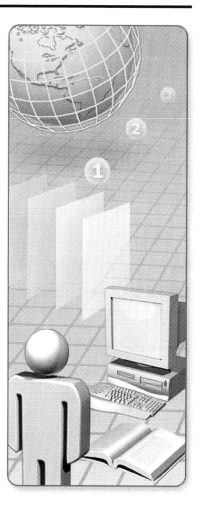

Information in this document, including URL and other Internet Web site references, is subject to change without notice. Unless otherwise noted, the example companies, organizations, products, domain names, e-mail addresses, logos, people, places, and events depicted herein are fictitious, and no association with any real company, organization, product, domain name, e-mail address, logo, person, place or event is intended or should be inferred. Complying with all applicable copyright laws is the responsibility of the user. Without limiting the rights under copyright, no part of this document may be reproduced, stored in or introduced into a retrieval system, or transmitted in any form or by any means (electronic, mechanical, photocopying, recording, or otherwise), or for any purpose, without the express written permission of Microsoft Corporation.

Microsoft may have patents, patent applications, trademarks, copyrights, or other intellectual property rights covering subject matter in this document. Except as expressly provided in any written license agreement from Microsoft, the furnishing of this document does not give you any license to these patents, trademarks, copyrights, or other intellectual property.

© 2003 Microsoft Corporation. All rights reserved.

Microsoft, MS-DOS, Windows, Windows NT, Windows Server 2003, Active Directory, MSDN, Windows Media, and Windows Server are either registered trademarks or trademarks of Microsoft Corporation in the United States and/or other countries.

The names of actual companies and products mentioned herein may be the trademarks of their respective owners.

Overview

- Terminal Server Licensing
- Lab: Managing Terminal Services
- Lab Discussion
- Best Practices

Microsoft® Windows Server™ 2003 introduces many new Terminal Server features. These include licensing updates, controlling configuration with Group Policy, and redirection features.

This unit will introduce these new features, discuss how to configure them, and provide steps to help you troubleshoot problems.

Objectives

After completing this unit, you will be able to:

- Install Terminal Services.
- Install Terminal Server Licensing.
- Configure Terminal Services.
- Manage user sessions by using Terminal Services Manager.

 Additional Information For more information about Terminal Services, see the white paper *Technical Overview of Terminal Services*, under Additional Reading on the Web page on the Student Materials compact disc.

Terminal Server Licensing

Windows Server 2003 Terminal Server Licensing changes include:
- New TS User CAL
- New TS-EC, which replaces Terminal Server Internet Connector
- Removing operating system equivalency

The Terminal Server Licensing transition plan entitles customers to:
- A Windows Server 2003 TS CAL with SA coverage - for each desktop with either platform or operating system component EAs, UA, or SA coverage
- A Windows Server 2003 TS CAL without upgrade rights - for each licensed desktop without upgrade rights

***

Microsoft is introducing new Terminal Server Licensing options with Windows Server 2003 to address customer business needs and to complement the technical capabilities of Windows Server 2003. The new options will be particularly beneficial to those who seek user-based licensing, those who would like to provide server access to their customers or business partners, or those who run solutions that use multiple Microsoft server products.

Terminal Server Licensing Changes

The following list describes the changes to Terminal Server Licensing in Windows Server 2003:

- New Terminal Server user-based CAL

    Microsoft is introducing a new type of Terminal Server Client Access License (TS CAL). In addition to the existing Terminal Server device-based CAL (TS Device CAL), Windows Server 2003 Terminal Server will also offer a user-based CAL—TS User CAL. By having two types of TS CALs, you are able to use the model that is more economical for your organization. For example, purchasing a TS User CAL might make more sense if your company has a need for employees to have Terminal Server access from multiple devices. TS Device CALs may be preferable if your company has workers who share devices.

- New Terminal Server External Connector License option

    Terminal Services in Windows Server 2003 will offer a new External Connector (EC) license—the Terminal Server External Connector (TS-EC)—to permit external users to access a company's terminal servers, without the need to purchase individual TS CALs for them or their devices. An example of an external user is a person who is not an employee of the company or its affiliates.

    TS-EC in Windows Server 2003 replaces the Terminal Server Internet Connector license in Microsoft Windows® 2000.

Note Companies can purchase TS CALs for external entities, such as business partners, to give those entities access to their terminal servers. This may be the best solution when a small number of business partners need access to a terminal server or group of terminal servers.

- Removing operating system equivalency in Terminal Server

  With Windows 2000 Terminal Server Licensing, if a client device is running the most recent version of Windows, a TS CAL is not required to satisfy the licensing requirement. However, with Windows Server 2003, a TS CAL will be required for each device or user using the Terminal Server functionality, regardless of which desktop operating system is on the computer.

Terminal Server Licensing Transition Plan

Microsoft realizes that the removal of operating system equivalency in Terminal Server will affect its existing customers. To accommodate existing Microsoft customers who would like to take advantage of Windows Server 2003 features, Microsoft is offering a transition plan.

Every Windows XP Professional license that customers own on the date of the public launch of Windows Server 2003 will be eligible for a Windows Server 2003 TS CAL. One of following scenarios will apply:

- Customers with either the platform or the operating system component Enterprise Agreements (EAs), or Upgrade Advantage (UA), or Software Assurance (SA) coverage for their computers running Windows will be eligible for a Windows Server 2003 TS CAL plus SA coverage on that TS CAL for each covered desktop owned at the time of the Windows Server 2003 launch.

- Customers who own Windows XP Professional licenses, without upgrade rights—no EAs, SA, or UA—will be eligible for a Windows Server 2003 TS CAL for each licensed desktop owned at the time of the Windows Server 2003 launch, but will not get upgrade rights on the TS CAL.

 Additional Information For more information about Terminal Server Licensing upgrades in Windows Server 2003, see the Support WebCast, "*Microsoft Windows Server 2003 Terminal Services: New Features*" at http://support.microsoft.com/default.aspx?scid=/servicedesks/webcasts/wc121702/wcblurb121702.asp.

Lab: Managing Terminal Services

In this lab, you will:
- Install Terminal Services
- Install Terminal Server Licensing
- Configure Terminal Services

After completing this lab, you will be able to:
- Install Terminal Services.
- Install Terminal Server Licensing.
- Configure Terminal Services.

Toolbox Resources

If necessary, use one or more of the following Toolbox resources to help you complete this lab:

- Using the Manage Your Server Wizard to Install Terminal Services
- Installing Terminal Server Licensing
- Best Practices for Implementing Terminal Services
- Using the Remote Desktop Users Group to Provide Access to Terminal Servers
- Using Group Policy to Configure Terminal Services

Estimated time to complete this lab: **45 minutes**

Exercise 1
Installing and Managing Terminal Services

In this exercise, you will install and configure Terminal Services.

Tasks	Supporting information
1. Install Terminal Services.	■ Ensure that operating system components are installed according to company policy. See the Toolbox resource, Using the Manage Your Server Wizard to Install Terminal Services.
2. Install Terminal Services Licensing.	■ **Tip:** To access the **Run As** dialog box for **Add or Remove Programs**, press SHIFT, right-click **Add or Remove Programs**, and then click **Run As**. See the Toolbox resource, Installing Terminal Server Licensing.
3. Configure Terminal Services so that only members of the Sales organization and Administrators have access.	See the following Toolbox resources: ■ Best Practices for Implementing Terminal Services ■ Using the Remote Desktop Users Group to Provide Access to Terminal Servers
4. Configure an appropriate encryption level for Terminal Services connections. Keep in mind that not all clients have the latest Remote Desktop Client installed.	■ The following encryption levels are available: • High • Client Compatible • Low ■ Decide which approach is the best solution, and then implement it. You can use the space below to record your decision. Be prepared to explain your solution. _____ _____ _____ _____ See the Toolbox resource, Using Group Policy to Configure Terminal Services.
5. Configure Terminal Services to ensure that users have access to their local drives when connecting to the Terminal Server.	See the Toolbox resource, Using Group Policy to Configure Terminal Services.

(*continued*)

Tasks	Supporting information
6. Configure Terminal Services to ensure that users have access to their local printers when connecting to the Terminal Server.	See the Toolbox resource, Using Group Policy to Configure Terminal Services.
7. Configure Terminal Services to ensure that if a client is disconnected, they attempt to reconnect automatically, and, if the connection is successful, that they reconnect to the same session, and not create a new session.	See the Toolbox resource, Using Group Policy to Configure Terminal Services.
8. To help control the load on the Terminal Server, make sure that each user can have only one session active.	See the Toolbox resource, Using Group Policy to Configure Terminal Services.
9. Configure Terminal Services so that administrators can remotely control all sessions without requiring permission from a user.	See the Toolbox resource, Using Group Policy to Configure Terminal Services.
10. Test the configuration changes.	- **Tip:** Use **Remote Desktop Connection** to connect to your own Terminal Server to test the configuration changes.

Lab E-mail

From: Maria Hammond

To: Systems Administrators

Sent: Thu Sep 04 15:27:08 2003

Subject: Terminal services project

We are ready to move ahead with our Terminal Services deployment. The Terminal Services deployment team has identified the following requirements for the roll-out:

1. Terminal Services will be used to support remote access to NorthWind Trader's line of business applications.
2. As with our entire network infrastructure, the Terminal Services deployment must be as secure as possible.
3. A number of the users who will be accessing the Terminal Servers will be working with documents that are stored on their local hard drives They must be able to access those documents when connected to the Terminal Servers.
4. Those users who have locally attached printers must be able to print to their local printers when connected to the Terminal Servers.
5. The following configuration settings are required on all Terminal Servers:
   - Clients that are disconnected must automatically attempt to reconnect.
   - Each user must be restricted to a single Terminal Server connection.
   - Administrators must be able to remotely control all sessions without first requiring permission from the user.
6. Only members of the Sales organization will be allowed access to the Terminal Servers during the first phase of the roll-out.

Keep in mind that although the initial deployment will consist of only a single Terminal Server, the plan calls for the deployment of 100 Terminal Servers. As you are aware, we strive for efficiency at NorthWind Traders, so be sure to keep that in mind when implementing the requirements.

One other thing, our deployment of Windows XP has fallen behind schedule due to a lack of resources. So unfortunately, we still have some computers that are not running the latest version of the Remote Desktop client software. I'm not sure how this will impact you, but I wanted to make you aware of this.

Maria Hammond, MCSE

Network Manager

NorthWind Traders, Inc.

Lab Discussion

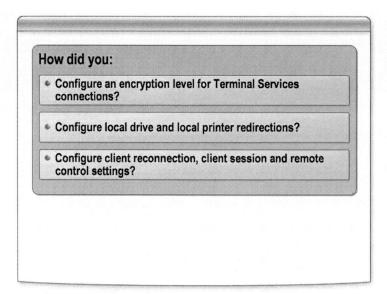

Discuss with the class how you implemented the solutions in the preceding lab. During this discussion, explain why you chose a particular solution.

- How did you configure an encryption level for Terminal Services connections? Did you use:
  - High?
  - Client Compatible?
  - Low?
- How did you configure Terminal Services to ensure that:
  - Users accessing the terminal servers are able to access documents stored on their local hard drives when connected to the terminal servers?
  - Users who have locally attached printers are able to print to their local printers when connected to the terminal servers?
- How did you configure Terminal Servers to ensure that:
  - Clients that are disconnected must automatically attempt to reconnect?
  - Each user must be restricted to a single Terminal Server connection?
  - Administrators are able to remotely control all sessions without first seeking permission from the user?

Best Practices

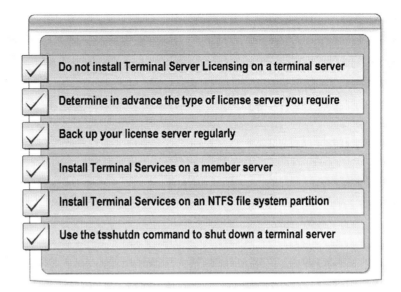

- You should install Terminal Server Licensing on a computer that is not a terminal server.

  Terminal servers allow unlicensed clients to connect for 120 days from the date of the first client logon. After this evaluation period ends, a terminal server can no longer allow clients to connect unless it locates a Terminal Server License Server to issue client licenses.

- Before installing the license server, determine which of two types of license servers that you require—a domain license server or an enterprise license server.

  By default, a license server is installed as an enterprise license server.
  - An enterprise license server is appropriate if your network includes several domains.
  - A domain license server is appropriate if you want to maintain a separate license server for each domain.

     Note Terminal servers can access domain license servers only if they are in the same domain as the license server. If your network includes workgroups or Windows NT 4.0 domains, the domain license server is the only type of license server that you can install and use.

- Back up your license server regularly.

  Backing up your license server regularly protects data from accidental loss. Create a duplicate copy of the data on your hard disk and then archive the data on another storage device, such as a removable disk or tape. In the event that the original data on your hard disk is accidentally erased or overwritten, or becomes inaccessible because of a hard disk failure, you can easily restore the data from the archived copy.

- Install Terminal Services on a member server and not on a domain controller.

  Installing Terminal Services on a domain controller can affect the performance of the server because of the additional memory, network traffic, and processor time required to perform the tasks of a domain controller in a domain.

- Install Terminal Services on an NTFS file system partition.

    NTFS provides greater security for users in a multisession environment who access the same data structures.

- When shutting down a terminal server, use the **tsshutdn** command instead of the **Shut Down** option on the **Start** menu.

    Using the **tsshutdn** command will shut down the server in a controlled manner. The **Shut Down** option on the **Start** menu does not notify users before ending user sessions and is not recommended. Ending a user's session without warning can result in loss of data at the client.

Unit 8: Managing IIS 6.0 Web Services

Contents

Overview	1
What's New in IIS 6.0?	2
What are Application Pools?	4
Lab: Installing and Managing IIS 6.0 Web Services	6
Lab Discussion	11
Best Practices	12
Workshop Evaluation	14

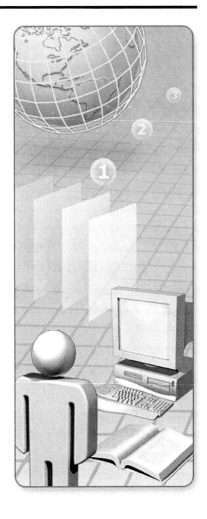

Information in this document, including URL and other Internet Web site references, is subject to change without notice. Unless otherwise noted, the example companies, organizations, products, domain names, e-mail addresses, logos, people, places, and events depicted herein are fictitious, and no association with any real company, organization, product, domain name, e-mail address, logo, person, place or event is intended or should be inferred. Complying with all applicable copyright laws is the responsibility of the user. Without limiting the rights under copyright, no part of this document may be reproduced, stored in or introduced into a retrieval system, or transmitted in any form or by any means (electronic, mechanical, photocopying, recording, or otherwise), or for any purpose, without the express written permission of Microsoft Corporation.

Microsoft may have patents, patent applications, trademarks, copyrights, or other intellectual property rights covering subject matter in this document. Except as expressly provided in any written license agreement from Microsoft, the furnishing of this document does not give you any license to these patents, trademarks, copyrights, or other intellectual property.

© 2003 Microsoft Corporation. All rights reserved.

Microsoft, MS-DOS, Windows, Windows NT, Windows Server 2003, Active Directory, MSDN, Windows Media, and Windows Server are either registered trademarks or trademarks of Microsoft Corporation in the United States and/or other countries.

The names of actual companies and products mentioned herein may be the trademarks of their respective owners.

Overview

- What's New in IIS 6.0?
- What are Application Pools?
- Lab: Installing and Managing IIS 6.0 Web Services
- Lab Discussion
- Best Practices

All operating systems in the Microsoft® Windows Server™ 2003 family include a new version of Internet Information Server (IIS). IIS 6.0 includes many security, reliability, and management enhancements. Although many of the management tasks for systems administration have not changed since earlier versions of IIS, there are some new tasks resulting from new features. Additionally, there are new tools, such as a new remote administration tool and command-line administration scripts, that systems administrators will use to install and manage IIS 6.0.

Objectives

After completing this unit, you will be able to:

- Install and configure IIS 6.0.
- Install ASP.NET.
- Implement Web applications.
- Implement application pooling.
- Manage an IIS 6.0 server.
- Manage an IIS server in a remote location.
    - Enable an IIS server for remote administration.
    - Install the Remote Administration (HTML) utility.
    - Connect by using the IIS Manager snap-in.
    - Connect by using the Administration Web site.
- Configure security for a Web site.

 Additional Information For more information about IIS 6.0, see the white paper *Technical Overview of Internet Information Services (IIS) 6.0*, under Additional Reading on the Web page on the Student Materials compact disc.

What's New in IIS 6.0?

- **Application isolation modes**
  - Worker process isolation mode
  - IIS 5.0 isolation mode
- **Security enhancements**
  - Not installed by default
  - Installs in a secure mode; delivers only static content
  - Supports multiple authentication methods
  - IIS 6.0 runs as a low privileged account
  - Recognized file extensions
- **Application support**
  - Application pools
  - ASP.NET support
- **New IIS 6.0 tools**
  - IIS Manager
  - Remote Administration (HTML) Tool
  - Command-line administration scripts

IIS 6.0—available in all versions of the Windows Server 2003 family—includes a number of new features and capabilities that can help increase the reliability, manageability, scalability, and security of a Web application infrastructure.

 Additional Information For more information about the new features in IIS 6.0, see "What's Changed" in the IIS 6.0 Help, which is located in Windows Server 2003 Help and Support.

Application Isolation Modes

IIS 6.0 provides the following two modes of operation—whose internal workings are fundamentally different—in which to configure your application environment.

- *Worker process isolation mode.* This mode isolates key components of the World Wide Web Publishing Service (WWW service) from the effects of defective applications and protects applications from each other by using isolated worker processes. In this mode, you can isolate individual Web applications or Web sites in a self-contained process (memory space) that is separate from other processes that contain other applications or Web sites. After a clean install of IIS 6.0, IIS runs in worker process isolation mode by default.

- *IIS 5.0 isolation mode.* In this mode, application processes are managed in a similar fashion to the process management in IIS 5.0. This ensures compatibility for existing IIS applications. After upgrading from IIS 5.0 or IIS 4.0, IIS 6.0 runs in IIS 5.0 isolation mode by default to maintain compatibility with existing applications.

It is not possible to run some Web applications in worker process isolation mode and others in IIS 5.0 isolation mode on the same application server. If you have applications that require separate modes, you must run them on separate computers.

 Additional Information For more information about the IIS 6.0 architecture, see "IIS 6.0 Architecture" in the IIS 6.0 Help, which is located in Windows Server 2003 Help and Support.

Security Enhancements

- *IIS 6.0 is not installed by default on Windows Server 2003.* Administrators must explicitly install IIS and IIS-related services.

- *IIS 6.0 installs in a secure mode.* When you initially install IIS, the service installs in a highly secure and "locked" mode. The default installation of IIS exposes only minimal functionality. Only static files get served. All other functionality, such as Active Server Pages (ASP), ASP.NET, WebDAV publishing, and FrontPage Server Extensions, must be enabled by an administrator.

- *Expanded authentication support.* In addition to integrated Windows authentication, basic authentication, digest authentication, and client certificates, IIS 6.0 is now capable of authenticating users by using .NET Passports.

- *IIS runs as a low privileged account by default.* The worker process runs as the NetworkService account, which is a new built-in account with very few privileges. Running as a low privileged account reduces security vulnerability because the worker process has very few rights on the underlying system.

- *Recognized file extensions.* IIS only serves requests to files that have recognized file extensions and rejects requests to file extensions that it does not recognize. Administrators configure which file extensions are recognized by IIS.

Application Support

- *Application pooling.* An *application pool* is a configuration that links one or more Web applications to a worker process. By creating new application pools and assigning applications to them, you can ensure that applications in one application pool are not affected by problems caused by applications in other application pools. This ensures that your Web applications remain available.

- *Support for ASP.NET applications.* ASP.NET is a Web application platform that provides the services necessary to build and deploy Web applications and XML Web services. ASP.NET is available and is installed, by default, on the operating systems in the Windows Server 2003 family.

New IIS 6.0 Tools

- *IIS Manager.* The redesigned MMC snap-in for configuring and managing IIS 6.0.

- *Remote Administration (HTML) Tool.* Allows administrators to use a Web browser to remotely administer a Web server across an intranet or across the Internet.

- *Command-line administration scripts.* IIS 6.0 includes supported scripts in the Windows\System32 directory that you can use to administer an IIS 6.0 Web server. By using these scripts, you can do many of the most common tasks facing a Web administrator from the command-line without having to use a user interface.

 Additional Information For more information about command-line administration scripts, see "Using Command-Line Administration Scripts" in the IIS 6.0 Help, which is located in Windows Server 2003 Help and Support.

What are Application Pools?

- **Application pools are groupings of applications that share the same worker process (W3wp.exe)**
  - The worker process for one pool is separated from the worker process of a different pool
  - An application that fails in one pool does not affect applications running in other pools
- **Application pools:**
  - Are available only in worker process isolation mode
  - Allow unique configuration settings for each pool
  - Run under an account that has minimal user rights
- **Follow guidelines for creating application pools**

You can separate different Web applications and Web sites by isolating them into pools, called application pools. An *application pool* is a grouping of URLs that are linked to one or more worker processes that share the same configuration.

Every application within an application pool shares the same worker process. Because each worker process operates as a separate instance of the worker process executable, W3wp.exe, the worker process that services one application pool is separated from the worker process that services another. This ensures that if a Web application fails, it will not affect the applications that are running in other application pools. By default, applications are assigned to the default application pool, which is named DefaultAppPool.

Application pools:

- Are available only when IIS 6.0 is running in worker process isolation mode.
- Allow you to set specific configuration settings that are applied to groups of applications and the worker processes servicing those applications.
- Run under the NetworkService account, by default, which has low-level user access rights. Running an application pool under an account with increased user rights presents a high security risk.

To implement application pools, you:

1. Create a new application pool.

2. Assign applications to the application pool.

Guidelines for Creating Application Pools

- Isolate Web applications on a Web site from Web applications on other sites running on the same computer. To do this, create an individual application pool for each Web site.

- If you want to configure an application to run with its own unique set of properties, create a separate application pool for that application.

- For enhanced security, configure a unique user account for each application pool; configure this account with the least user rights possible. The identity of an application pool is the name of the account under which the application pool's worker process runs. By default, application pools operate under the Network Service account, which has low-level user access rights. Running an application pool under an account with increased user rights presents an increased security risk.

- Separate the test and production version of the same application running on the same server by placing them in different application pools.

- To conserve memory, minimize the number of application pools.

Lab: Installing and Managing IIS 6.0 Web Services

In this lab, you will:
- Install and configure IIS 6.0
- Implement application pools
- Backup and restore a Web server
- Remotely manage a Web server

After completing this lab, you will be able to:

- Install and configure IIS 6.0.
- Implement application pools.
- Backup and restore a Web server.
- Remotely manage a Web server.

Toolbox Resources

If necessary, use one or more of the following Toolbox resources to help you complete this lab:

- Installing IIS 6.0 by Using Manage Your Server
- Creating an IIS 6.0 Configuration Backup
- Using the Remote Administration (HTML) Tool to Manage a Web Server
- Installing Applications into IIS 6.0
- Creating an Application Pool and Assigning an Application
- Restricting Access to Groups by Using Web.Config
- The Differences Between Using Manage Your Server and Add/Remove Programs to Install IIS 6.0
- Using .Config Files
- Restoring an IIS 6.0 Configuration Backup
- Installing the Remote Administration (HTML) Tool

Estimated time to complete this lab: **60 minutes**

Exercise 1
Installing and Managing IIS 6.0

In this exercise, you will install, configure, and manage IIS 6.0. You will also create an application pool and assign an application to it.

Tasks	Supporting information
1. Log on as Administrator to ensure that you have sufficient privileges to configure IIS. Add the Application Server role by using Manage Your Server to install IIS 6.0. Be sure to enable ASP.NET as you add the role.	See the following Toolbox resources: ■ Installing IIS 6.0 by Using Manage Your Server ■ The Differences Between Using Manage Your Server and Add/Remove Programs to Install IIS 6.0
2. Install the Human Resources ASP.NET application to C:\inetpub\wwwroot\hrapp\ • Files for the application are located in the Human Resources Apps folder under Network Files. • Make the application available in the /**hrapp**/ virtual directory in IIS.	See the Toolbox resource, Installing Applications into IIS 6.0.
3. Create the **Pre-Production** and **Production** application pools. Assign the Human Resources application to the **Pre-Production** pool.	See the Toolbox resource, Creating an Application Pool and Assigning an Application.
4. Restrict application access to members of the Human Resources group.	■ To restrict access to the Human Resources group, you could: • Use NTFS file permissions • Edit the Web.config file ■ Decide which approach is the best solution, and then implement it. You can use the space below to record your decision. Be prepared to explain your solution. _____ _____ _____ _____ See the following Toolbox resources: ■ Using .Config Files ■ Restricting Access to Groups by Using Web.Config

(*continued*)

Tasks	Supporting information
5. Install the Remote Administration (HTML) Tool.	See the Toolbox resource, Installing the Remote Administration (HTML) Tool.
6. Back up the Web server configuration.	See the Toolbox resource, Creating an IIS 6.0 Configuration Backup.
7. Create a Web site at C:\Websites\Temporary\ using the site identifier **Temporary**. In the next step, you will restore this Web site to verify that backup and restore functions work correctly.	▪ To create the Temporary Web site, you could: • Use the Internet Information Services (IIS) Manager snap-in • Use the Remote Administration (HTML) tool ▪ Decide which approach is the best solution, and then implement it. You can use the space below to record your decision. Be prepared to explain your solution. _____ _____ _____ _____ See the Toolbox resource, Using the Remote Administration (HTML) Tool to Manage a Web Server.
8. Restore the Web server configuration to return IIS to the configuration that you backed up in Step 6. Verify that the Temporary Web site has been removed.	See the Toolbox resource, Restoring an IIS 6.0 Configuration Backup.

Lab Configuration Task

You need to prepare your computer for the next unit by removing the Application Server role by using Manage Your Server.

Task	Detailed steps
1. Remove the Application Server role by using Manage Your Server.	a. Open Manage Your Server, and then click **Add or remove a role**. b. In the Configure Your Server Wizard, click **Next**. c. On the **Server Role** page, select **Application Server**, and then click **Next**. d. On the **Role Removal Confirmation** page, select **Remove the application server role**, and then click **Next**. e. After the wizard has completed, click **Finish**.

Lab E-Mail

From: Maria Hammond

To: Systems Administrators

Sent: Thu Sep 04 15:46:45 2003

Subject: Human Resources Web-based application roll-out

You'll find the new HR application in the Human Resources Apps folder under Network Files.

To support this application, you must deploy IIS 6.0 and meet the following requirements:

- The IIS installation must be as secure as is possible.
- The Web server must support ASP.NET.
- Only members of the Human Resources department will be allowed to access this application.
- Both the IIS server and the application must be backed up on a regular basis, and you must test both the backup and restore functions before moving the application from the Pre-Production to the Production application pool.
- The Web server must be enabled for remote management from a Web browser.

Please let me know when you're done.

Maria Hammond, MCSE

Network Manager

NorthWind Traders, Inc.

Lab Discussion

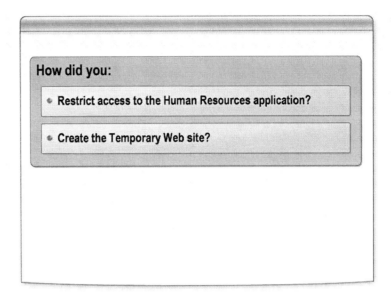

Discuss with the class how you implemented the solutions in the preceding lab. During this discussion, explain why you chose a particular solution.

- How did you restrict access to the Human Resources application to only members of the Human Resources group? Did you:
  - Use NTFS file permissions?
  - Edit the Web.config file?
- How did you create the Temporary Web site? Did you:
  - Use IIS Manager?
  - Use the Remote Administration (HTML) tool?

Best Practices

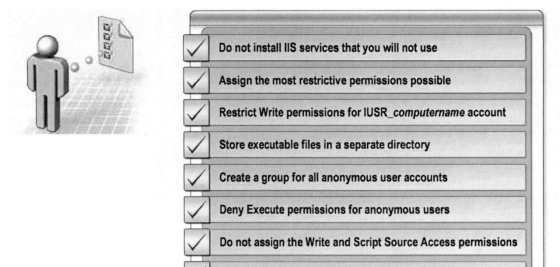

- To reduce the attack surface, do not install IIS services that you will not use.

    This includes IIS-related services such as File Transfer Protocol (FTP), Network News Transfer Protocol (NNTP), or Simple Mail Transfer Protocol (SMTP).

- Assign the most restrictive permissions possible.

    For example, if your Web site is used only for viewing information, assign only Read permissions. If a directory or site contains applications, assign Scripts Only permissions instead of Scripts and Executables permissions.

- Restrict Write permissions for the IUSR_*computername* account.

    This will help limit the access that anonymous users have to your Web servers.

- Store executable files (.exe files) in a separate directory.

    This makes it easier to assign access permissions and to audit access to these files.

- Create a group for all anonymous user accounts.

    You can deny access permissions to resources based on this group membership.

- For anonymous users, deny Execute permissions to the system files that are not required by the application.

- Do not assign a combination of the Write permission and the Script Source Access permission. Additionally, do not assign the Scripts and the Executables permission.

    Use this combination of permissions with extreme caution. It can allow a user to upload potentially harmful executable files to your server and run them. For more information, see "About Web Site Permissions" in IIS 6.0 Help, which is located in Windows Server 2003 Help and Support.

- Use IP address restrictions if administering IIS remotely.

    You can configure your Web site to grant or deny specific computers, groups of computers, or domains access to Web sites, directories, or files. For example, if your intranet server is connected to the Internet, you can prevent Internet users from accessing your Web server by granting access only to computers connected to your intranet, and explicitly denying access to outside users.

 Additional Information For more information about using IP address restrictions, see "Securing Sites with IP Address Restrictions" in the IIS 6.0 Help, which is located in Windows Server 2003 Help and Support.

Workshop Evaluation

Your evaluation of this workshop will help Microsoft understand the quality of your learning experience.

At a convenient time before the end of the workshop, please complete a workshop evaluation, which is available at http://www.CourseSurvey.com.

Microsoft will keep your evaluation strictly confidential and will use your responses to improve your future learning experience.

Unit 9: Maintaining Software by Using Software Update Services

Contents

Overview	1
Multimedia: Software Update Services	2
Requirements for SUS	3
Lab: Maintaining Software by Using Software Update Services	5
Lab Discussion	9
Best Practices	10

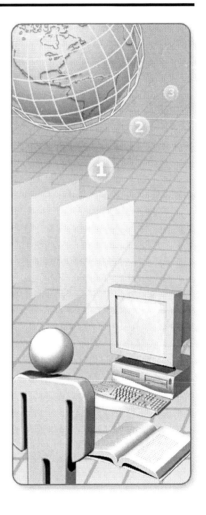

Information in this document, including URL and other Internet Web site references, is subject to change without notice. Unless otherwise noted, the example companies, organizations, products, domain names, e-mail addresses, logos, people, places, and events depicted herein are fictitious, and no association with any real company, organization, product, domain name, e-mail address, logo, person, place or event is intended or should be inferred. Complying with all applicable copyright laws is the responsibility of the user. Without limiting the rights under copyright, no part of this document may be reproduced, stored in or introduced into a retrieval system, or transmitted in any form or by any means (electronic, mechanical, photocopying, recording, or otherwise), or for any purpose, without the express written permission of Microsoft Corporation.

Microsoft may have patents, patent applications, trademarks, copyrights, or other intellectual property rights covering subject matter in this document. Except as expressly provided in any written license agreement from Microsoft, the furnishing of this document does not give you any license to these patents, trademarks, copyrights, or other intellectual property.

© 2003 Microsoft Corporation. All rights reserved.

Microsoft, MS-DOS, Windows, Windows NT, Windows Server 2003, Active Directory, MSDN, Windows Media, and Windows Server are either registered trademarks or trademarks of Microsoft Corporation in the United States and/or other countries.

The names of actual companies and products mentioned herein may be the trademarks of their respective owners.

Overview

- **Multimedia: Software Update Services**
- **Requirements for SUS**
- **Lab: Maintaining Software by Using Software Update Services**
- **Lab Discussion**
- **Best Practices**

Microsoft® Software Update Services (SUS) is a tool for managing and distributing software updates that resolve known security vulnerabilities and other stability issues in Microsoft Windows® 2000, Windows XP, and Windows Server™ 2003 operating systems.

By using SUS, you gain control over the distribution of critical Windows updates to client computers on your network. You can quickly download the latest critical updates, test them in your environment, and then deploy them to computers on your network.

Objectives

After completing this unit, you will be able to:

- Install and configure SUS on a server.
- Configure automatic updates.
- Use Group Policy to configure SUS clients.
- Manage a software update infrastructure.
- Test an SUS implementation.

Multimedia: Software Update Services

- This presentation provides a high level overview of how Software Update Services simplifies the process of keeping Windows-based systems up-to-date with the latest critical updates

Traditionally, systems administrators keep systems up-to-date by frequently checking the Windows Update Web site or the Microsoft Security Web site for software updates. Administrators manually download available updates, test the updates in their environment, and then distribute the updates manually or by using their traditional software-distribution tools.

By using Software Update Services, administrators can perform these tasks automatically.

 Note To access the Software Update Services presentation, open the Web page on the Student Materials compact disc, click Multimedia, and then click the title of the presentation. After you open the multimedia presentation, press F11 to view it in full-screen mode.

Requirements for SUS

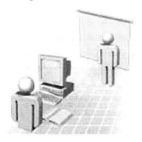

- **Hardware requirements**
  - Pentium III 700 MHz or higher
  - 512 MB of RAM
  - 6 GB of hard disk space for setup and security packages
- **Software requirements**
  - Windows 2000 Server with Service Pack 2 or later, or Windows Server 2003
  - IIS 5.0 or later
  - Internet Explorer 6.0 or later
- **Disk requirements**
  - Software Update Services software must be installed on an NTFS partition

***

You install the server component of SUS by using a Windows Installer package that installs the necessary server files and configures Internet Information Services (IIS). To ensure that your server can support SUS, check the hardware and software capabilities of your server. Setup will not allow you to install SUS if your computer does not meet the following minimum requirements.

Hardware Requirements

A server running SUS requires the following hardware:

- Pentium III 700 megahertz (MHz) or higher
- 512 megabytes (MB) of RAM
- 6 gigabytes (GB) of hard disk space for setup and security packages

A server with the preceding hardware running SUS can support approximately 15,000 clients.

Software Requirements

A server running SUS requires the following software:

- Windows 2000 Server with Service Pack 2 or later, or Windows Server 2003
- IIS 5.0 or later
- Internet Explorer 6.0 or later

Disk Requirements

In addition to the preceding hardware and software requirements, the SUS software must be installed on an NTFS partition on the server. The system partition on your server must also use NTFS, because FAT32 does not offer security.

 Additional Information For more information about server requirements for Software Update Services, see the white papers, *Software Update Services Overview*, and *Deploying Software Update Services*, under **Additional Reading** on the Web page on the Student Materials compact disc.

Lab: Maintaining Software by Using Software Update Services

In this lab, you will:
- Install and configure SUS on a server
- Configure automatic updates
- Use Group Policy to configure SUS clients
- Manage a software update infrastructure
- Test an SUS implementation

After completing this lab, you will be able to:

- Install and configure SUS on a server.
- Configure automatic updates.
- Use Group Policy to configure SUS clients.
- Manage a software update infrastructure.
- Test an SUS implementation.

Toolbox Resources

If necessary, use one or more of the following Toolbox resources to help you complete this lab:

- Installing IIS 6.0 by Using Manage Your Server
- Installing Microsoft Software Update Services
- Configuring a Microsoft Software Update Services Server
- Configuring Automatic Synchronization of a Microsoft Software Update Services Server
- Configuring Automatic Updates Clients by Using Group Policy
- Manually Synchronizing a Microsoft Software Update Services Server
- Approving Microsoft Software Update Services Updates
- Backing Up a Microsoft Software Update Services Server
- Restoring a Microsoft Software Update Services Server

Estimated time to complete this lab: **45 minutes**

Exercise 1
Installing and Configuring Microsoft Software Update Services

In this exercise, you will install and configure SUS, manually approve updates, and verify the backup and restore of the SUS server.

Tasks	Supporting information
1. Install Internet Information Services (IIS).	- SUS does not require ASP.NET or Front Page Extensions. See the Toolbox resource, Installing IIS 6.0 by Using Manage Your Server.
2. Install Microsoft Software Update Services (SUS) by using the following parameters: • Setup file location: \\london\setup • Setup file name: Sus10sp1.exe • SUS Web site files location: C:\SUS • SUS updates location: C:\SUS\Content • Accept updates in all languages. • Manually approve new versions of previously approved updates.	See the Toolbox resource, Installing Microsoft Software Update Services.
3. Configure SUS to synchronize with the Glasgow SUS server daily at 13:00.	- **Note:** If you have problems accessing the SUS administration Web site, please read the note in the Installing Microsoft Software Update Services Toolbox resource. See the following Toolbox resources: - Configuring a Microsoft Software Update Services Server - Configuring Automatic Synchronization of a Microsoft Software Update Services Server

(*continued*)

Tasks	Supporting information
4. Configure Automatic Updates for all clients in your domain by using the following parameters: • Automatically download and install new updates daily at 04:00. • Download updates from the domain controller for your domain. • Send statistics to the Glasgow server. • Do not automatically restart after installing updates.	See the Toolbox resource, Configuring Automatic Updates Clients by Using Group Policy.
5. Manually synchronize your server with the Glasgow server.	See the Toolbox resource, Manually Synchronizing a Microsoft Software Update Services Server.
6. After the synchronization process is complete, approve any new updates.	See the Toolbox resource, Approving Microsoft Software Update Services Updates.
7. Verify that you can successfully back up and restore SUS.	▪ To be certain that a backup and restore will work, you should uninstall SUS and IIS, reinstall IIS and SUS, and then test your backup. See the following Toolbox resources: ▪ Backing Up a Microsoft Software Update Services Server ▪ Restoring a Microsoft Software Update Services Server

Lab E-mail

From: Maria Hammond

To: Systems Administrators

Sent: Fri Sep 05 11:04:28 2003

Subject: Installing SUS

Install SUS on your domain controller. The installation file is located on \London\Setup. SUS must support all available languages. Set it up it so you manually approve new versions of approved updates. When you configure it, have it synchronize from the Glasgow server instead of directly from the Microsoft Windows Update servers. Glasgow has already been configured to get the updates once a day at noon. Configure your server to check for new updates every day one hour after that. Configure all of the clients in your domain so they:

- Automatically install new updates every day at 4:00 AM.
- Use your server as their update source.
- Send update statistics to the Glasgow server.
- Do not restart automatically if new updates are installed.

When you synchronize your server, you should see some test packages - go ahead and approve those to make sure everything is updating properly. When it is, please back up the SUS server.

Maria Hammond, MCSE

Network Manager

NorthWind Traders, Inc.

Lab Discussion

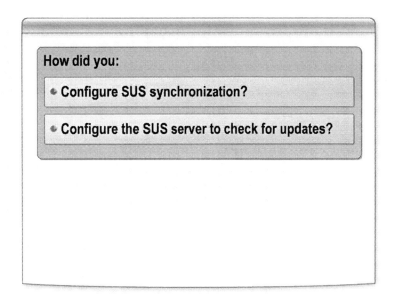

Discuss with the class how you implemented the solutions in the preceding lab. During this discussion, explain why you chose a particular solution.

- How did you configure SUS synchronization? Did you configure SUS to:
  - Synchronize with Microsoft Windows Update servers?
  - Synchronize with a test server set up to get updates?
- How did you configure the SUS server to check for updates? Did you set up the SUS server to check for:
  - Automatic updates?
  - Manual approval of updates?

Best Practices

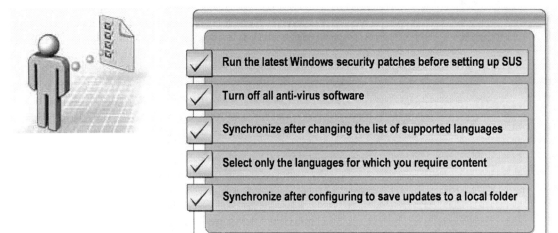

- Before setting up a server to run SUS, ensure that the server is already running the latest Windows security patches.

    Make sure that the server is running the latest service pack, security rollup package, and security-related patches, and that the computer is virus-free.

- When installing SUS on a server, turn off all antivirus software.

    You do this to make sure that the antivirus software does not mistake the SUS installation as virus activity. After the installation is complete, turn on the antivirus software.

- If you change the list of languages that you support, you should immediately synchronize SUS.

    Synchronizing SUS immediately after changing the list of supported languages will download the appropriate packages for the locales that you may have added.

- If you host content locally, select only the languages for which you require content.

    This will greatly reduce the amount of content that you must synchronize. For example, if all of your computers use English and German languages, select only English and German; only these packages will be downloaded.

- If you change your SUS configuration from **Maintain the updates on a Microsoft Windows Update server** to **Save the updates to a local folder**, immediately synchronize SUS.

    Synchronizing SUS immediately after configuring to save updates to a local folder will download the necessary packages to the location that you have selected.

Unit 10: Managing Disaster Recovery

Contents

Overview	1
Multimedia: Shadow Copies of Shared Folders	2
What Is Automated System Recovery?	3
Lab: Managing Disaster Recovery	4
Lab Discussion	8
Best Practices for Backing Up Data	9
Best Practices for Restoring Data	11
Workshop Evaluation	12

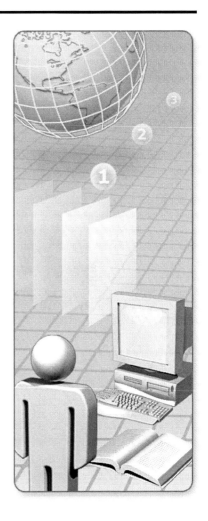

Information in this document, including URL and other Internet Web site references, is subject to change without notice. Unless otherwise noted, the example companies, organizations, products, domain names, e-mail addresses, logos, people, places, and events depicted herein are fictitious, and no association with any real company, organization, product, domain name, e-mail address, logo, person, place or event is intended or should be inferred. Complying with all applicable copyright laws is the responsibility of the user. Without limiting the rights under copyright, no part of this document may be reproduced, stored in or introduced into a retrieval system, or transmitted in any form or by any means (electronic, mechanical, photocopying, recording, or otherwise), or for any purpose, without the express written permission of Microsoft Corporation.

Microsoft may have patents, patent applications, trademarks, copyrights, or other intellectual property rights covering subject matter in this document. Except as expressly provided in any written license agreement from Microsoft, the furnishing of this document does not give you any license to these patents, trademarks, copyrights, or other intellectual property.

© 2003 Microsoft Corporation. All rights reserved.

Microsoft, MS-DOS, Windows, Windows NT, Windows Server 2003, Active Directory, MSDN, Windows Media, and Windows Server are either registered trademarks or trademarks of Microsoft Corporation in the United States and/or other countries.

The names of actual companies and products mentioned herein may be the trademarks of their respective owners.

Overview

- **Multimedia: Shadow Copies of Shared Folders**
- **What Is Automated System Recovery?**
- **Lab: Managing Disaster Recovery**
- **Lab Discussion**
- **Best Practices for Backing Up Data**
- **Best Practices for Restoring Data**

The business world depends on mission-critical electronic data more than ever. As a result, organizations are placing a premium on protecting their information technology (IT) assets from data loss and server failure. *Disaster recovery* is the process of resuming normal business operations as quickly as possible after a disaster ends.

Microsoft® Windows Server™ 2003 includes new features and improvements to prevent data loss and to recover from data losses after they occur. Understanding these features is essential to developing and implementing an effective disaster protection and recovery plan.

This unit discusses the following Windows Server 2003 features that help manage disaster recovery:

- *Volume Shadow Copy service:* A general infrastructure for creating point-in-time copies of data on a volume. These are generally referred to as snapshots. The purpose of the Volume Shadow Copy service is to provide an efficient, robust, and useful mechanism for the next generation of data management applications.

- *Automated System Recovery (ASR)*: A new feature in Windows Server 2003, ASR improves productivity by enabling one-step restoration of the operating system, system state, and hardware configuration in disaster recovery situations.

Objectives

After completing this unit, you will be able to:

- Use ASR to back up and restore a server.
- Restore data from shadow copies.
- Troubleshoot problems associated with restoring data.

Multimedia: Shadow Copies of Shared Folders

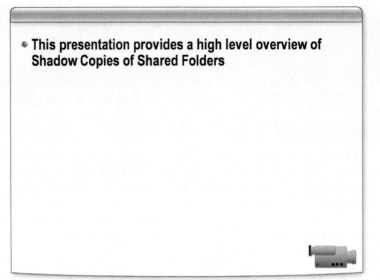

- This presentation provides a high level overview of Shadow Copies of Shared Folders

Volume Shadow Copy service provides an infrastructure for creating a point-in-time copy of a single volume or multiple volumes. Used for managing data from directly attached storage to storage area networks (SAN), Volume Shadow Copy service coordinates with business applications, backup applications, and storage hardware to enable data management.

In addition, the Volume Shadow Copy service enables Windows-based client computers to view and recover previous versions of their files without IT intervention, resulting in greater productivity at lower costs. The Volume Shadow Copy service is enabled on a server by using Shadow Copies of Shared Folders, and on a client computer by installing the Previous Versions Client software.

 Note To access the Shadow Copies of Shared Folders presentation, open the Web page on the Student Materials compact disc, click Multimedia, and then click the title of the presentation. After you open the multimedia presentation, press F11 to view it in full-screen mode.

What Is Automated System Recovery?

- A recovery option in the Backup utility that contains two parts: ASR backup and ASR restore
- Can back up the operating system
- Does not include data files
- Creates a floppy disk, which contains information about:
  - Backup location data
  - Disk configurations (including basic and dynamic volumes)
  - How to accomplish a restore procedure

 Automated System Recovery Wizard
The ASR Preparation wizard helps you create a two-part backup of your system: a floppy disk that has your system settings, and other media that contains a backup of your local system partition.

- Choose the All information on this computer option; it will back up all data including System State data

---

Automated System Recovery (ASR), located in the Backup utility, helps you recover a system that does not start. ASR contains two parts: backup and recovery.

ASR does the following tasks to manage disaster recovery situations:

- ASR restores the operating system.

  Typically, after installing or upgrading to Windows Server 2003, you create an ASR backup set. The ASR process enables you to restore an installation of Windows Server 2003 to the condition of the operating system at the time that you created the ASR backup set.

- The ASR Preparation Backup Wizard backs up the System State data, system services, and all disks that are associated with the operating system components, but does not back up data files.

- ASR also creates a floppy disk that stores disk configurations during the ASR restore procedure. The ASR floppy disk contains information about:

  - The backup location
  - The disk configurations, including basic and dynamic volumes
  - The restore procedure

Backup or Restore Wizard

An ASR backup set, when created by using the ASR Preparation Backup Wizard, does not back up data files. However, if you use the **Backup or Restore Wizard**, and select the **All information on this computer** option, all data on the computer, in addition to the System State data, and the operating system components are backed up. This option also creates an ASR floppy disk that you can use to restore Windows in case of a complete system failure.

Lab: Managing Disaster Recovery

In this lab, you will:
- Use ASR to back up and restore a server
- Restore data from shadow copies
- Troubleshoot problems associated with restoring data

After completing this lab, you will be able to:

- Use ASR to back up and restore a server.
- Restore data from shadow copies.
- Troubleshoot problems associated with restoring data.

Toolbox Resources

If necessary, use one or more of the following Toolbox resources to help you complete this lab:

- Configuring Shadow Copies of Shared Folders
- Using Shadow Copies of Shared Folders from a Client Computer
- Best Practices for Configuring Shadow Copies of Shared Folders on the Server
- Using ASR to Back Up and Restore a Server

Estimated time to complete this lab: **45 minutes**

Exercise 1
Preparing for Disaster Recovery

In this exercise, you will prepare for disaster recovery by using shadow copies of shared folders and ASR.

Tasks	Supporting information
1. Enable and configure shadow copies so that the C:\Projects folder is protected. Store the shadow copies data on the D drive. After you have enabled and configured shadow copies, verify that you can restore a deleted file from the Projects share.	See the following Toolbox resources: - Configuring Shadow Copies of Shared Folders - Using Shadow Copies of Shared Folders from a Client Computer - Best Practices for Configuring Shadow Copies of Shared Folders on the Server - **Tip:** To verify that you can restore a deleted file from the Project share, you must access the shared folder by using a universal naming convention (UNC) path.

2. Back up the server so that it can be restored in the shortest amount of time possible. Store the backup file on the D drive. Make sure that in addition to the operating system files and disk configuration, you also back up the data in the C:\Projects folder.	- To complete this requirement, you could:
	  • Create an Automated System Recovery backup set by using the Backup or Restore Wizard.
	  • Create an Automated System Recovery backup set by using the Automated System Recovery Wizard, and back up the C:\Projects folder separately.
	  • Back up the operating system files and the System State data in one backup set, and then back up the C:\Projects folder in a different backup set.
	- Decide which approach is the best solution, and then implement it. You can use the space below to record your decision. Be prepared to explain your solution.
	
	_____
	_____
	_____
	_____
	
	See the Toolbox resource, Using ASR to Back Up and Restore a Server.

Exercise 2
Troubleshooting Disaster Recovery

In this exercise, you will troubleshoot a restore operation.

Issue	Supporting information
1. You are logged on as MoseleyJ with a password of P@ssw0rd. You attempt to restore the backup file C:\Program Files\Microsoft Training\2209\Labfiles\Unit10\Backup.bkf. You are unable to complete this task.	▪ For more information, see "Permissions and user rights required to back up and restore" in the Windows Server 2003 documentation.

Lab E-mail

From: Maria Hammond

To: Systems Administrators

Sent: Fri Sep 05 11:32:14 2003

Subject: Backup and shadow copy

Sorry to be so scattered earlier. Here's the list of what I'd like you to do:

1. Enable the shadow copy feature so the C:\Projects directory is protected. Store the shadow copy data on the D drive.
2. Backup the server so that it can be restored in the shortest amount of time possible. The C:\Projects data is the only data on the server that needs to be backed up. Create the backup file on the D drive.

Thanks!

Maria Hammond, MCSE

Network Manager

NorthWind Traders, Inc.

Lab Discussion

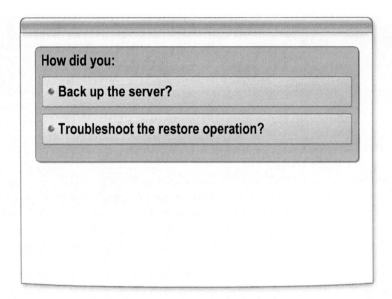

Discuss with the class how you implemented the solutions in the preceding lab. During this discussion, explain why you chose a particular solution.

- How did you back up the server? Did you:
  - Create an Automated System Recovery backup set by using the Backup or Restore Wizard?
  - Create an Automated System Recovery backup set by using the Automated System Recovery Wizard, and back up the C:\Projects folder separately?
  - Back up the operating system files and the system state data in one backup set, and then back up the C:\Projects folder in a different backup set?
- How did you troubleshoot the restore operation? Did you have the required permissions and user rights to restore the backup file?

Best Practices for Backing Up Data

- ✓ Create a disaster recovery plan
- ✓ Test your backup files and your backup plan
- ✓ Keep two sets of backed-up files
- ✓ Create a backup of the System State data
- ✓ Install the Recovery Console as a startup option
- ✓ Keep the installation CD-ROM available
- ✓ Enable auditing of backup events
- ✓ Separate the backup and restore roles

- Create a disaster recovery plan for performing regular backup operations.

    Review and incorporate a plan for backing up all of your files on a regular basis. Keep a log of every update in your disaster recovery plan.

- Test your backup files and your backup plan.

    Testing your backup files and recovery plan is an important part of being prepared for disaster recovery. Testing must include the following tasks:

    - Test your uninterruptible power supply (UPS) on the computers running Windows Server 2003 and on hubs, routers, and other network components.
    - Perform full or partial restorations from your daily, weekly, and monthly backup media.

- Keep two sets of backed-up files: one on-site, for accessibility, and one off-site, for security.

    The backup should be accessible, such as on network shared folders or removable media, in case the data must be restored to another computer.

    If possible, make a copy of your backup sets every day and store them at both on-site and off-site locations. That way, if a catastrophic event, such as a fire, destroys all of your computers and on-site backup sets, you can restore all your data later. However, if all of your backups are off-site, every time you need to recover a file, you must get the backup files from the off-site location.

- Create a backup of the System State data.

    Create a backup copy of the System State data in the unlikely event that the hard disk on the server fails and cannot be recovered. This copy can help you restore your operating system to a new hard disk.

- Install the Recovery Console.

  Install the Recovery Console on your computer to make it available in case you are unable to restart Windows Server 2003. You can then select the Recovery Console option from the list of available operating systems in safe mode.

- Keep the installation CD-ROM available.

  Keep the installation CD-ROM where you can find it easily. You can start the computer from the CD-ROM and then use the Recovery Console or Automated System Recovery.

- Enable auditing of backup events.

  Auditing backup events allows you to ensure that only authorized backups are being performed.

- Separate the backup and restore roles.

  Separating the backup and restore roles ensures that a single person cannot both back up and restore data.

Best Practices for Restoring Data

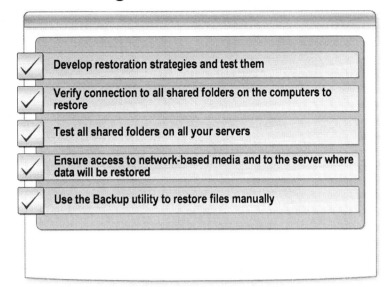

- ✓ Develop restoration strategies and test them
- ✓ Verify connection to all shared folders on the computers to restore
- ✓ Test all shared folders on all your servers
- ✓ Ensure access to network-based media and to the server where data will be restored
- ✓ Use the Backup utility to restore files manually

- Develop restoration strategies and test them.

    Remember to keep a record of your backup and restoration plans to refer to in the event of data loss.

- Verify that you can connect to all shared folders on other computers that must be restored.

    You can use the default user rights of the Backup Operators group to restore your organization's data and system files, or you can segregate backup and restore permissions by groups.

- Test all shared folders on all servers for which you are responsible.

    This will ensure that you can restore data contained in them.

- Ensure that you have access to network-based media and to the server where the data will be restored.

    As part of your restoration plan, be sure that you test your access to the storage media where you backed up your files.

- To restore files manually, use the Backup utility and select the appropriate files or folders.

    Because you may need to restore only certain files, test the procedure that you will use to select and restore only those files, using the Backup utility.

Workshop Evaluation

Your evaluation of this workshop will help Microsoft understand the quality of your learning experience.

To complete a workshop evaluation, go to http://www.CourseSurvey.com.

Microsoft will keep your evaluation strictly confidential and will use your responses to improve your future learning experience.

Appendix C: Network Files

The following sections contain the information from the network files in the Resource Toolkit.

Acceptable Use of Administrator and Non-Administrator Accounts

Users who perform administrative functions must undergo a thorough background check before receiving administrative access.

After an administrator has received authority for a server or domain, the administrator must change the Administrator account password. The password must be written down and stored in a sealed envelope in the secure vault to aid in disaster recovery. Access to these written passwords must be granted by at least three members of the security incident response team after an incident review. Any time the password is changed, the old password must be discarded and the new one placed in the vault.

An administrator may log on with the Administrator account only to perform a task that cannot be accomplished with the secondary logon service. For example, it is not possible to run Windows Explorer by using Run As. If the user account does not have sufficient rights or permissions, users may perform those tasks while logged on as Administrator. After completing these tasks, the user must immediately log off and log on by using the non-administrative account.

Failure to comply with these policies can result in disciplinary action as described in the employee handbook, Section IV, Failure to Comply With Company Security Policies.

Account Creation Policy

Account names are created by using the last name followed by one or more letters of the first name to establish a unique name. All new accounts must be disabled until the user reports for work on the first day. A complex password must be assigned by default.

Group Naming Policy

Each Group name must follow the guidelines contained in this policy and include the following information about the group:

- Type of group

    The group name must begin with an identifier from the following list:
    - G for a Global group
    - U for a Universal group
    - L for a Domain local group
    - LL for Local groups

- Location: Following the type of group, include the first three characters of the location.

- User or resource type
- Access level, if applicable

The following Group names were created by using the naming guidelines:

- **G MON DB Managers** for the Global Montreal Database Managers.
- **L PAR DB Read** for the Domain Local Paris Database Read Only group.

Do not use local groups on member servers or workstations unless you receive written permission from the administrative access group.

Operating System Components Installation Policy

New configuration of server roles must be approved by the Infrastructure Design team.

Whenever possible, all new installations of operating system components must be performed by using Manage Your Server. If it is not possible to install a component by using Manage Your Server, you are required to obtain and follow the appropriate procedure from the Infrastructure Design team to ensure proper configuration.

Any server reconfigurations that require system reboots must be performed during scheduled maintenance times.

Security Baseline Configuration Policy

Each system must meet the following security baseline configuration guidelines:

- Domain controllers must use the hisecdc template with the following modifications:
  - The Print Spooler service must be disabled.
  - The Telnet service must be disabled.
- External IIS servers must use the customized appserverext template. Internal IIS servers must use the customized appserverint template. These templates are based on the iesacles template.
- File servers must use the hisecws template.
- Workstations must use the hisecws template.
- Desktop computers must be running Windows 2000 Professional or Windows XP.
- Laptops must be running the customized hisec_lap template.

Notes

Notes

Notes

Notes

MSM2209BCPWKBK/C90-02043